THE CURRY BOOK

THE
CURRY
BOOK

A Celebration of Memorable Flavors and Irresistible Recipes

Nancie McDermott

Illustrations by
PAULINE CILMI SPEERS

CHAPTERS™

CHAPTERS PUBLISHING LTD., SHELBURNE, VT 05482

Published by Chapters Publishing, Ltd., 2085 Shelburne Road, Shelburne, VT 05482

Library of Congress Cataloging-in-Publication Data

McDermott, Nancie.

The curry book: a celebration of memorable flavors and irresistible
recipes / by Nancie McDermott; illustrations by Pauline Cilmi Speers.

p.   cm.

Includes bibliographical references and index.

ISBN 1-57630-029-3 (softcover)

1. Cookery (Curry)   I. Title.

TX819.C9M37 1997

641.6'384—DC21   96-37467

Printed and bound in Canada by
Best Book Manufacturers, Inc.

Designed by Susan McClellan

To my beloved husband,

William Tsung-Liang Lee,

who makes life sweet as palm sugar,

spicy as Thai mussamun curry,

cool as cucumber raita

and satisfying as a plate of jasmine rice

ACKNOWLEDGMENTS

I AM DEEPLY GRATEFUL to the people who helped me as I wrote this book. My thanks to Phillis Carey, Jill O'Connor and Kelley Worrell, superb professional cooks, for their excellent work in helping me bring these recipes to the page, and to Fiona Urquhart for her patient, astute and insightful editorial attention to the manuscript. I also thank Sherrie Doren, Karen Spangler, Tracy Norton, Leticia Oregon, Caroll Hesseltine and Hye Suk Knapp, gifted teachers, for keeping my sweet daughters, Camellia and Isabelle, happy while I worked.

CONTENTS

INTRODUCTION

THIS IS A BOOK FOR PEOPLE WHO share my passion for curries, spices and fragrant herbs, for intense and memorable flavors and for recipes that bring a taste of faraway places to the home kitchen. I fell in love with curries and curry flavors during the three years I spent as a Peace Corps volunteer in Thailand, teaching English in an up-country junior-high school. Born and raised in North Carolina, I arrived in Thailand with a typical Southerner's culinary sensibility: an abiding affection for good food and a rather limited appreciation of spices and herbs.

Nothing prepared me for the magnificent mosaic of curry flavors that are at the heart of Thai cuisine. Settling down in the small town of Thatoom in the northeastern province of Surin, I was soon enchanted by the array of delicious curries presented to me. I was also amazed by the ease with which my neighbors prepared these dishes, tossing a handful of whole spices into a dry skillet to toast them and chopping a small bouquet of fragrant herbs into a heavenly confetti.

Each curry started with a lump of moist, intensely flavorful paste made from fresh herbs and roasted spices. Called *krueng gaeng* in Thai, these pastes often contain prodigious amounts of chili peppers and make use of fresh lemongrass, a cousin of ginger called galanga, cilantro root and a few spices—usually whole cumin, coriander and white or black peppercorns. *Gaeng* means curry, and *krueng* means engine, expressing precisely how these pastes make curries "go," igniting their dazzling flavors like the key to a car.

My favorite of these building blocks was green curry paste, whose tiny yet incendiary fresh green chili peppers fire up an incomparable chicken curry, studded with tiny eggplants the size of peas. I also adored a spectacular thickly sauced curry of thinly sliced beef, which was enriched with ground peanuts and adorned with a flourish of wild lime leaves and fresh basil. I eagerly accepted invitations to Thai weddings, Buddhist ordinations, christenings and housewarmings, in part because I could count on being served a fabulous mussamun curry, made with beef, potatoes and peanuts and a mélange of spices, including cinnamon, cloves, nutmeg and cardamom. Many of my fellow Peace Corps volunteers shared my mania, and together we searched out Thailand's signature curries while immersing ourselves in Thai life.

Three years later, when I returned home to North Carolina, I found that my universe had been permanently expanded, and I longed for the curry flavors that had lit up my plate during my time in Thailand. I decided to figure out how to re-create the bright flavor of curries in my own kitchen, using ingredients and utensils I could find near at hand. As a junior-high Social Studies and English teacher in the Piedmont, I was fortunate to have many students whose families had settled in that region as refugees in the aftermath of the Vietnam War. With only a hint or two from me, my students invited me home for dinner, and there I found generous-hearted teachers to guide me in my exploration of the curry dishes of Laos, Cambodia, Thailand and Vietnam.

IN THEIR HOMELANDS, my Southeast Asian friends had only to step into their yards to gather fresh lemongrass, wild lime leaves, coconuts and chili peppers from which to craft the evening's curry. Transplanted to America, they skillfully adapted their dishes, using vegetables, herbs and spices found in the supermarket, and they became adept at procuring certain other ingredients, such as canned coconut milk, prepared curry paste, fish sauce and tamarind, from a local Asian market. Using this bounty, they connected their kitchens to the countries they had left behind.

In addition to peering over my friends' shoulders as they cooked, I turned to countless superb books on the cuisines of India and Thailand to learn the basics of curries and related dishes. As I simmered endless variations on the spice-infused theme, I experimented, modifying recipes as necessary, according to the time and the ingredients available to me. My growing repertoire duplicated the flavors I remembered, while conforming to the demands of a busy North American schedule and a family more concerned about when dinner will be ready and how it tastes than whether it is authentic. As I worked, I was struck by the myriad ways in which cooks from Senegal to Jamaica, Tokyo to Jakarta and Sri Lanka to Syd-

ney have reinterpreted this Asian concept, just as I was doing in my own kitchen.

LIKE CURRIES IN THE REST of the world, the Thai curries that originally inspired me have their roots in the dazzling and complex cuisine of India. This legacy reflects centuries of ongoing contact between India and the kingdoms of Southeast Asia, created by a thriving trade in spices and other precious goods throughout the ancient world. Within a few hundred years of the birth of Christ, sailing ships followed trade winds to Southeast Asian waters, traveling to and from ports in India as well as Europe, Africa and the Middle East. The spread of Buddhism, Hinduism and Islam during this period also served to transmit an abundance of Indian cultural traditions to what are now the nations of Indonesia, Malaysia, Singapore, Thailand, Burma, Cambodia and Laos, where they took root and flourish to this day.

To create their curries, Indian cooks

make patient, expert use of an astounding array of whole spices, toasting and grinding them into fragrant powders known as dry masalas, and mashing them up with ginger, onion, cilantro and chilies into moist seasoning pastes called wet masalas. Southeast Asian cooks seized on the concept of wet masalas with a passion, streamlining them to reduce the role of spices and amplify the herbs.

The migration of curries continued through the centuries, whenever and wherever large numbers of Indian immigrants settled around the world. During the British Raj, two waves of workers sowed the seeds of Indian culinary traditions in countries under British rule throughout Africa, Southeast Asia and the Caribbean Islands. Following the outlawing of slavery by the British in the early 1800s, countless Indian nationals were sent to labor on colonial plantations as indentured servants. Other Indians went to colonial outposts worldwide as civil servants, administering the British Empire as it increased in strength and size. It was during this period that the prepared blend called curry powder, previously unknown, was created, largely for expatriates who were fond of India's complex spices but lacked the desire to explore the dazzling universe of that country's culinary arts.

Invariably, as the Indian culinary traditions traveled further afield, they were simplified, as cooks adopted, adapted and reinterpreted, with Sri Lankans toasting their whole spices to a deeper brown, while ratcheting up the chili-pepper quotient to incendiary levels, and Caribbean Islanders grinding homegrown allspice berries into their powders and adding wine or a splash of rum to fortify a sauce.

FOR THE HOME COOK, this tradition of borrowing means that curry can be as easy as you want it—made with store-bought preparations—or as traditional—ground in your own kitchen from heady herbs and spices. Curry powder offers convenience and accessibility, whittling down some of the complexities of Indian spices into a familiar ingredient, providing predictable results with a minimum of effort and time. Classic blends usually include cumin, coriander, peppercorns, chilies, mustard seeds and fenugreek, with turmeric providing the familiar golden hue. When I am in a hurry, I rely on jars of curry powders and ground spices plucked from a supermarket spice rack, or on the excellent traditional-style pastes and powders found in gourmet markets, specialty-food shops and Asian grocery stores. When I have more time, I make my own. I keep a little collection of jars on my shelf, both homemade creations and prepared curry powders from India, the United States, Malaysia, Singapore and Jamaica.

THE RECIPES IN THIS BOOK travel beyond the borders of any one culinary tradition. Many are simple, designed to be ready in the time it takes rice or pasta to cook. Some, such as Deviled Eggs with Cilantro and Curry (page 36) or Vegetable Ravioli with Toasted Walnuts in Curry Cream Sauce (page 144), are untraditional. Others re-create an authentic dish, such as Green Pea Curry with Fresh Paneer Cheese (page 150) — a classic Indian vegetarian dish — or Thai Mussamun Curry with Chicken, Potatoes and Peanuts (page 105), like the one I tasted during my Peace Corps days. You will also find plenty of chutneys and cool relishes to pair with curry dishes, as well as recipes for rice, flatbreads and even beverages to round out the meal.

All the following recipes can be made either with prepared curry powders and curry pastes or with those created from scratch. You can substitute one paste for another with abandon, bearing in mind that Thai pastes have a drier texture and contain more herbs, fewer spices and usually considerably more chili heat than most commercial Indian pastes. Thai pastes include mussamun, panaeng, green, red and yellow — the colors refer to the hue of the chilies and spices used rather than to that of the finished dish.

In many recipes, curry paste can also be substituted for curry powder. If you use Thai paste, you will need to add a generous dash of ground turmeric if you want the signature sunny color. However, I do not recommend substituting curry powder for paste, since the powder lacks herbaceous complexity. Mail-Order Sources (page 257) refer you to a fine armchair bazaar of merchants who will gladly ship curry's exotic components right to your door.

To make the dishes in this book, you can rely on the standard equipment of a typical Western kitchen. You will need a cutting board, a paring knife and a good chef's knife or cleaver for chopping. A small frying pan for roasting spices and a large, deep frying pan for sautéing aromatic vegetables, cooking flatbreads and making many curry dishes will serve you well, backed up by a generous saucepan or two in the 2-to-3-quart range. A good rice cooker is a wise investment if you love rice as much as I do, since it relieves you of the chore of precisely timing it, while freeing up a spot on your stovetop.

If you want to make your own curry pastes and powders, you will need another tool or two. You can grind whole spices in a standard electric coffee grinder, but be sure to buy a separate one for this job, as aromas and flavors linger tenaciously and will add an overly exotic note to your morning brew. A mini food processor or a blender will help you make short work of curry pastes. Start with finely chopped ingredients, stop to scrape down the sides as you work, and add water or oil little by little as needed to move the blades. My large food processor leaves fibrous lemongrass, galanga and ginger in chunks too big to suit me, but experiment with the equipment you have to come up with a paste you like.

If you take pleasure in following a traditional path, search out a mighty granite mortar and pestle imported from Thailand to use for grinding spices and pastes. The weight of the pestle allows you to pulverize whole spices in about the same amount of time it takes to use an electric grinder, but it calls for both patience and elbow grease. Look for Thai-style mortars and pestles in the equipment aisle in Southeast Asian markets or check Mail-Order Sources (page 257). You can also order handsome Middle Eastern-style spice grinders from vendors listed in that section.

To create your own pastes and powders, you may want to follow the lead of the Thais and open your kitchen to friends. Thai kitchens are gathering places, where several generations of women come together to share the chores and lighten the burdens of cooking. Children yank on their parents, to be lifted up or pacified with a snack, while music floats under a cloud of conversation, opinions and laughter, punctuated by the sounds of chopping and running water and the comforting perfume of culinary works in progress. And at the end, everyone has a few jars of curry gold to carry home.

For me, the simple act of grinding and mixing has another benefit. It continues the spice route, keeping me connected to my days in Thailand, to my friends and family far and near, and to cooks in far-away places I can only visit on the map.

S<small>UGGESTED</small> M<small>ENUS</small>
for C<small>URRY</small>
A<small>FICIONADOS</small>

Y<small>OU MAY PREFER TO SPIKE</small> an everyday menu with a lively curry dish or two, but if you crave curry flavors, here are ideas for your table. These menus serve 4 to 6, excepting those noted "for a crowd," which serve 8 to 10. All recipes are to be found in this book, except for those marked with an asterisk.

Asian Curry Buffet *for a* Crowd

Crispy Lamb Wontons . . . 32

Cilantro Mint Chutney . . . 189

Singapore Curry Noodles with Green Peppers and Shrimp . . . 114

Tandoori Chicken Homestyle . . . 98

New Delhi Garbanzos . . . 156

Jasmine Rice . . . 165

Lemon Sorbet with Ginger Cookies*

Orange Sections*

Indian Curry Dinner

Cucumber Raita . . . 197

Chicken Curry . . . 94

Fresh Mango Chutney . . . 196

Basmati Rice . . . 163

Green Salad with Vinaigrette*

Indian Vegetarian Curry Dinner

Banana Tamarind Chutney . . . 188

Green Pea Curry with Fresh Paneer Cheese . . . 150

Dal . . . 146

Yellow Rice Pilaf with Whole Spices *or* Pooris . . . 168 or 182

Thai Curry Dinner

Shrimp Satay with Thai-Style Peanut Sauce . . . 38

Sweet and Sour Cucumber Salad . . . 202

Thai Red Curry with Beef, Eggplant and Red Bell Pepper . . . 132

Jasmine Rice . . . 165

Thai Vegetarian Curry Dinner

Carrot, Zucchini and Green Pepper Sticks* with
Thai-Style Peanut Sauce . . . 38
New Potatoes and Red Bell Peppers in Fresh Green Curry . . . 142
Fresh Fig Chutney . . . 190
Jasmine *or* Basmati Rice . . . 165 or 163

Vegetarian Luncheon *for a* Winter Day

Cheddar Curry Bites . . . 26
Curried Cream of Mushroom Soup . . . 52
Tossed Green Salad with Toasted Pine Nuts, Red Bell Pepper and Sunflower Sprouts*
Apple Crisp*

Vegetarian Dinner

Cream Cheese and Crackers* with Ginger Pear Chutney . . . 191
Curried Kabocha Pumpkin Soup . . . 50
Vegetable Ravioli with Toasted Walnuts in Curry Cream Sauce . . . 144
Butter Lettuce* with Tomato Cucumber Relish . . . 201
Fresh Fruit Tart*

Vegan Feast

Curried Fresh Corn Fritters . . . 28

Savory Curried Nuts . . . 41

Roots and Wings . . . 148

New Delhi Garbanzos . . . 156

Indonesian-Style Rice Pilaf . . . 164

Baked Apples*

Bridge Party Luncheon

Warm Brie* with Apple Raisin Chutney . . . 194

Curried Barbecued Chicken Salad with Rainbow Coleslaw and

Crispy Wonton Ribbons . . . 82

Curry Corn Bread Southern-Style . . . 180

Summer Berries with Crème Fraîche* or Lemon Tart*

Summertime Barbecue Feast

Curry Dip with Crudités . . . 23

Fresh Spinach Salad with Chutney Dressing . . . 68

Grilled Swordfish Steaks in Cilantro-Ginger Pesto . . . 120

Curried Couscous with Tomatoes and Zucchini . . . 174

Ice Cream Sundaes*

Curried Picnic *for a* Crowd

Deviled Eggs with Cilantro and Curry . . . 36

Tortilla Chips* with Tomato Cucumber Relish . . . 201

Honey-Curried Chicken Wings . . . 27

Shrimp and Sweet Corn Salad with Curried Avocado Aioli . . . **74 and 87**

New Potato Salad with Curry and Peas . . . 66

Fresh Lemongrass Cooler . . . 204

Elegant Dinner

Couscous-Stuffed Mushrooms . . . 24

Curried Scallops in Parchment Packages . . . 122

Rice Pilaf with Golden Onions, Cashews and Peas . . . 172

Steamed Asparagus with Lemon-Dill Butter*

Chocolate Mousse*

Cozy Winter Supper

Burmese-Style Pork Curry with Fresh Ginger . . . 126

Rice and Red Lentil Pilaf . . . 170

Chapatis . . . 176

Steamed Broccoli Florets*

Fruit-Filled Turnovers*

CHAPTER 1

APPETIZERS AND SNACKS

THE AROMAS AND FLAVORS of curry spices can weave magic, and this array of recipes is designed to get your party off to an enchanted start. From Couscous-Stuffed Mushrooms to Shrimp Satay with Thai-Style Peanut Sauce, from Curried Fresh Corn Fritters to Crispy Lamb Wontons, you will find nearly a dozen dishes to delight your guests and awaken their taste buds in the way that only curry can do.

Each of these recipes is abundantly seasoned with spicy flavors but without excessive chili pepper heat. With these accessible and inviting dishes, you can gently introduce guests with delicate palates to exotic spices. Those who like fiery foods can crank up the blaze in a flash by using additional curry seasonings, more chili peppers or a splash or two of five-alarm hot sauce.

All these dishes are finger food, making things easy whether you are hosting a stand-up gathering or inviting your guests to linger in the kitchen as you put finishing touches on the meal. By serving two or three of these appetizers together, you can create a lively dinner menu, simply adding a tossed green salad or a steamer of broccoli and carrots to round out the mix.

Many of the appetizers can be prepared partly or completely in advance and then whisked out for presentation as your first guests arrive. Curry Dip with

Crudités, Deviled Eggs with Cilantro and Curry, and Savory Curried Nuts all belong on your list of ready-when-you-are pleasers. Thai Curry Puffs, Honey-Curried Chicken Wings and Cheddar Curry Bites can be prepared in advance, set aside and placed in the oven to bake while you complete your preparations and greet your guests.

IF YOU ARE IN SEARCH OF A DISH to carry along to a potluck gathering, you will find good travelers here, guaranteed to win praise without a great deal of effort. Deviled Eggs with Cilantro and Curry seem to disappear regardless of whether the crowd is old or young, with tastes adventurous or timid. Other convenient carry-alongs include Thai Crab Meatballs with Sweet and Spicy Garlic Sauce, which reheat with ease. Curried Fresh Corn Fritters and Crispy Lamb Wontons are at their crunchy best hot from the oven, but they will still be delicious if you transport them on a foil-covered baking sheet and pop them into a warm oven to reheat once you arrive at your destination.

Appetizers *and* Snacks

CURRY DIP *with* CRUDITÉS

Makes 1 cup dip

A RAINBOW OF CRUDITÉS—fresh vegetables cut into bite-size or dipping-size pieces—makes a beautiful and healthful addition to any table. Grocery stores often carry precut vegetables—take advantage of them if you are short on time. Stir up this simple dip, surround it with the vegetables on a platter, and your edible centerpiece is ready when your guests arrive. This tastes best after at least an hour in the refrigerator and keeps well for up to 2 days.

¾ cup mayonnaise

¼ cup plain yogurt

2 teaspoons curry powder, store-bought or homemade *(page 222, 224 or 226)*

¼ teaspoon salt

2 green onions, finely chopped

2 tablespoons finely chopped fresh cilantro

Fresh vegetables, such as carrots, cucumbers, red bell peppers, broccoli florets and radishes

In a medium bowl, combine the mayonnaise and yogurt and stir well. Add the curry powder, salt, green onions and cilantro and stir again until well combined. Cover and chill for 1 hour or more.

Wash, trim and cut the vegetables into bite-size or dipping-size pieces. Arrange attractively on a platter along with a small bowl of curry dip and serve cold or cool.

COUSCOUS-STUFFED MUSHROOMS

Makes 16 pieces

PERFORM A MAGIC ACT AT YOUR NEXT GATHERING: Set out a batch of these curry-kissed mushrooms and watch them disappear!

½	cup water	2	teaspoons curry powder, store-bought or homemade *(page 222, 224 or 226)*
⅓	cup quick-cooking couscous		
½	teaspoon salt		
16	large mushrooms	2	tablespoons finely diced red bell pepper
3	tablespoons olive oil, *divided*		
3	green onions	¼	cup freshly grated Parmesan cheese

Preheat the oven to 400 degrees F.

In a small saucepan, bring the water to a rolling boil. Stir in the couscous and salt, cover and set aside for 5 minutes.

Meanwhile, wipe the mushrooms clean with a damp paper towel. Trim the ends from the stems and discard, snap out the stems and chop them very finely. Lightly grease the bottom of a 13-x-9-inch baking pan with 1 tablespoon of the oil and place the mushroom caps in the pan top sides down. Uncover the couscous, fluff it gently with a fork to separate the grains and set it aside.

Finely chop the green onions, separating the white portion from the green tops. Heat the remaining 2 tablespoons oil in a small frying pan over medium heat. Cook the chopped mushroom stems and white portion of the green onions for 1 minute. Add the curry powder, stirring to mix well. Continue cooking 3 minutes, stirring occasionally, until the mushrooms and onions are evenly coated and softened.

Transfer to a medium mixing bowl and add the couscous, chopped green onion tops and red pepper. Add the Parmesan cheese and toss to combine well.

Carefully stuff each mushroom cap with about 1 tablespoon of the filling. Bake for 12 to 15 minutes, until the mushrooms are tender and darkened. Serve warm or at room temperature.

NOTE

◉ If you prepare them in advance, cover the stuffed mushrooms and refrigerate until shortly before you are ready to bake them.

CHEDDAR **C**URRY **B**ITES

Makes 32 triangles

W HILE **C**HARLES **C**ARROLL, executive chef at The Balsams Grand Resort Hotel in Dixville Notch, New Hampshire, put finishing touches on an elaborate feast at the James Beard House in New York City, his guests made his simple starters disappear. You can toast the English muffins ahead of time, cover and chill, and then broil them just before serving for a hot, savory welcome to one and all.

1¾ cups grated Cheddar cheese	2 tablespoons curry powder,
2 green onions, minced	store-bought or homemade
1 can (2-ounce) sliced black	*(page 222, 224 or 226)*
olives, drained	4 English muffins, split and
¼ cup mayonnaise	toasted

Preheat the broiler.

In a medium bowl, toss together the cheese, green onions and olives.

In a small bowl, stir together the mayonnaise and curry powder. Add the curry mayonnaise to the cheese mixture, stirring and tossing to make a moist paste.

Divide the cheese mixture among the toasted English muffin halves and spread to cover the surface of each muffin evenly. Place the muffins on an ungreased baking sheet, cheese side up, and broil until they are puffed, hot and golden brown, 2 to 3 minutes. Cut each muffin into quarters and serve immediately.

Honey-Curried Chicken Wings

Makes about 28 pieces

PERFECT PARTY FOOD—simple to make, ready when you are and easy to eat. Try this marinade with chicken legs or thighs, and add more cayenne pepper, if you like.

4	tablespoons butter, melted	¼	teaspoon ground cayenne pepper
½	cup honey		
2	tablespoons Dijon mustard	½	teaspoon salt
2	tablespoons curry powder, store-bought or homemade *(page 222, 224 or 226)*	3	pounds chicken wings

Preheat the oven to 375 degrees F.

In a small bowl, combine the butter, honey, mustard, curry powder, cayenne and salt and stir well. Remove and discard the wing tips, or reserve for making stock.

Line a shallow baking pan with aluminum foil and place the wings in the pan in a single layer. Pour the sauce over them and toss to coat well. Roast until golden brown and cooked through, turning and basting twice, 45 to 50 minutes. Serve hot or warm.

NOTE

⊛ Sealed airtight, the wings keep 2 days in the refrigerator and several weeks in the freezer. Reheat at 350 degrees for 15 to 20 minutes.

CURRIED FRESH CORN FRITTERS

Makes 12 fritters

YOU WILL NEED THREE OR FOUR EARS OF CORN to make these tasty fritters. Make the Sweet and Sour Cucumber Salad in advance so that it will be crisp and cool. Add more curry paste to the fritters, if you like things extra spicy. You can substitute frozen kernels, thawed, when summer's corn is only a memory, or if you are in a rush.

2 cups fresh corn kernels,
   divided (3-4 ears)
1 large egg
½ cup flour
1 tablespoon yellow or red
   curry paste, store-bought or
   homemade *(page 216 or 218)*
2 tablespoons soy sauce

½ cup vegetable oil for frying
   Sweet and Sour Cucumber
   Salad *(page 202)*

In a food processor, combine 1 cup of the corn with the egg, flour, curry paste and soy sauce. Pulse to chop the corn and mix everything together well. Scrape the batter out into a bowl and stir in the remaining 1 cup corn.

Line a baking sheet with paper towels to hold the cooked fritters and place it next to the stove. In a medium frying pan, heat the oil over medium-high heat until a drop of batter sizzles as soon as it is added to the pan. Spoon about 2 tablespoons batter into the pan and flatten slightly to make a cake about 2 inches in diameter. Repeat, making 3 more cakes, spacing them 1 inch apart. Cook the cakes until they are golden brown on 1 side, 2 to 3 minutes. Turn carefully and cook until the second side is golden brown, 1 to 2 minutes more. Transfer to the paper-towel-lined baking sheet with a slotted spoon to drain.

Continue frying the fritters, 4 or 5 at a time, until all the batter is used. Serve hot or warm with Sweet and Sour Cucumber Salad.

NOTE

⊛ To reheat, place the fritters on a baking sheet and heat in a preheated 350-degree oven for 10 minutes. They will lose some crispness but still taste very good.

THAI CRAB MEATBALLS *with* SWEET *and* SPICY GARLIC SAUCE

Makes 25 to 30 meatballs

TAKE A BREAK FROM SWEET-AND-SOUR MEATBALLS with this curried Thai-inspired version. Like many of the traditional dumplings featured in Chinese dim-sum parlors, these appetizers combine seafood with ground meat. The rich flavor and sturdy, malleable texture of the pork fortifies the delicate crabmeat. The recipe calls for yellow curry paste, but use red or green if you like. To save time, you can substitute bottled plum sauce or sweet-and-sour sauce for dipping.

4 medium garlic cloves	½ pound crabmeat or 2 cans (each 6-ounce) crabmeat, well drained
2 tablespoons coarsely chopped fresh cilantro	
1 tablespoon yellow curry paste, store-bought or homemade *(page 216)*	½ pound ground pork or turkey
	1 large egg, lightly beaten
	About 1 cup flour
1 tablespoon fish sauce	2 tablespoons vegetable oil
1 tablespoon soy sauce	Sweet and Spicy Garlic Sauce *(page 232)*
½ teaspoon sugar	

In a small food processor or blender, combine the garlic, cilantro, curry paste, fish sauce, soy sauce and sugar. Grind to a fairly smooth paste, pulsing on and off and scraping down the sides to mix everything well.

In a medium bowl, combine the crab and pork or turkey. Add the paste and stir with a wooden spoon to mix well. Add the egg and stir again until the mixture is well combined. Shape the mixture into walnut-size balls, roll each lightly in flour, shake off the excess flour and set aside on a plate.

Next to the stove, place a plate lined with paper towels to drain the cooked meatballs. In a large frying pan, preferably nonstick, heat the oil over medium heat until a pinch of flour dropped into the oil sizzles at once. Carefully place about 10 meatballs in the hot oil and cook, turning occasionally to brown all sides evenly, until crispy, golden brown and cooked through, 3 to 5 minutes. Transfer to the paper-towel-lined plate to drain, and continue cooking the remaining meatballs. Serve hot with toothpicks and Sweet and Spicy Garlic Sauce for dipping.

NOTES

⊛ If you are preparing this dish more than 30 minutes in advance, cover the bowl and refrigerate the meat mixture until cooking time.

⊛ To check the meatballs for doneness, cut one in half to be sure the center is cooked through.

⊛ For an alternative way of serving this dish, make the meatballs into little lettuce tacos, placing each meatball on a small cup-shaped lettuce leaf and topping with a spoonful of dipping sauce and a sprig of fresh cilantro or mint. Leaves of Boston, butter, limestone or iceberg lettuce work well.

CRISPY LAMB WONTONS

Makes 30 wontons

STUFFING WONTON WRAPPERS with a curried lamb filling gives you a shortcut version of the savory Indian pastries called samosas. You can substitute ground pork, turkey or beef for the lamb. Make the filling far enough in advance so it can cool to room temperature before you shape the wontons.

2 tablespoons butter or vegetable oil	¾ pound ground lamb, pork or turkey
¾ cup finely chopped onion	1 teaspoon salt
1 tablespoon peeled, minced fresh ginger	2 teaspoons garam masala, store-bought or homemade (*page 228 or 230*)
1 teaspoon minced garlic	
1 teaspoon minced hot green chili pepper	2 tablespoons freshly squeezed lemon juice
½ teaspoon ground cumin	30 wonton wrappers
½ teaspoon ground turmeric	Vegetable oil for deep frying
⅛ teaspoon ground cayenne pepper	Ginger Pear Chutney (*page 191*) or store-bought chutney for dipping

To make the filling, heat the butter or oil in a large frying pan over medium heat. When it sizzles, add the onion, ginger, garlic and chili pepper and cook, stirring often, until everything is softened and the onion is golden, about 10 minutes. Stir in the cumin, turmeric and cayenne and toss well.

Crumble in the meat and salt and cook until the meat changes color, 1 to 2 minutes, stirring to break it up into tiny pieces. Reduce the heat to low, stir in the garam masala and lemon juice, and cook 5 minutes, stirring occasionally. Remove from the heat and set aside to cool to room temperature.

To form the wontons, place a small bowl of water and a baking sheet next to a dry cutting board where you will fill the wontons. Place a wonton wrapper on the cutting board with 1 point facing you, like a diamond. Moisten the 2 adjoining sides closest to you with water. Place 1 tablespoon of filling on the lower half of the wonton wrapper and fold the top point of the wrapper down to enclose the filling and make a plump triangle. Press the wet and dry edges together well to form a tight seal. Set aside on the baking sheet and continue filling the wonton wrappers, making sure to place the filled wontons so that they do not touch one another on the baking sheet.

To cook the wontons, place a baking sheet lined with paper towels next to the stove to hold the cooked wontons as they drain. In a wok or large, deep frying pan, heat about 3 inches vegetable oil to 350 degrees F. When a bit of wonton wrapper sizzles as soon as it is dropped into the pan, the oil is ready. Carefully lower 3 wontons into the oil and fry 2 to 3 minutes, turning once, until crisp and golden. Transfer to the paper-towel-lined baking sheet. Continue frying the remaining wontons. Serve hot or warm, alone or with Ginger Pear Chutney for dipping.

◀◀◀▶▶▶

NOTES

⊛ To reheat the wontons, place them on an ungreased baking sheet and heat at 375 degrees F for about 10 minutes, until hot in the center. They will lose some crispness but still taste very good.

⊛ You can freeze the wontons uncooked. Place them well apart on a baking sheet until frozen; transfer to an airtight container. Fry as directed without thawing, adding a minute or two.

THAI CURRY PUFFS

Makes 40 curry puffs

BUYING FROZEN PUFF PASTRY gives you a head start on these tasty triangles of curried minced turkey with potatoes and fresh cilantro. Try them for parties, when you need something hot with most of the work done well in advance. Fill and freeze until shortly before party time. Stick them into a hot oven, and present your first guests with a warm appetizer that only looks as though it took lots of time.

3 tablespoons vegetable oil, *divided*	¾ pound ground turkey
1 cup finely chopped onion	1 teaspoon sugar
1 cup peeled, finely chopped potato	1 teaspoon salt
2 tablespoons curry powder, store-bought or homemade *(page 222, 224 or 226)*	¼ cup chopped fresh cilantro
	1 package (17¼-ounce) frozen puff pastry dough, thawed
	1 egg, lightly beaten with 1 tablespoon water

To make the filling, heat 2 tablespoons of the oil in a large frying pan over medium-high heat. Add the onion and potato and cook, stirring often, until softened and fragrant, about 5 minutes.

Add the remaining 1 tablespoon oil to the pan along with the curry powder and cook for 30 seconds, tossing well. Add the turkey, sugar and salt and cook, stirring often, 4 to 5 minutes, until the turkey is cooked and the liquid is evaporated.

Remove from the heat, add the cilantro and toss well. Quickly transfer to a platter and spread out to cool to room temperature.

To make the curry puffs, preheat the oven to 400 degrees F. Line a baking sheet with parchment paper and set it aside.

Place 1 sheet of thawed puff pastry dough on a lightly floured board and roll it out into a rectangle 15 inches by 12 inches. Cut the pastry into twenty 3-inch squares. Spoon about 2 teaspoons of the turkey mixture onto each square. Using a pastry brush or a spoon, moisten 2 adjacent sides of each pastry square with the egg mixture. Fold them over to enclose the filling and form triangles, carefully pinching and stretching the dough as needed to seal them. Crimp the sealed edges with a fork and place the curry puffs on the parchment-lined baking sheet. Repeat with the remaining puff pastry sheet and filling.

Moisten the tops of the curry puffs with the egg mixture and bake 18 to 20 minutes until the puffs rise and turn a rich, golden brown. Serve hot or warm.

NOTE

⊛ You have several options for preparing these curry puffs in advance.

1. You can prepare the filling 1 day ahead. Once it has cooled to room temperature, cover and refrigerate it until you are ready to roll out and fill the puff pastry dough.

2. You can prepare the curry puffs, brush with the egg mixture and freeze them uncooked. Place them well apart on a baking sheet until frozen and transfer to an airtight container. To bake, transfer the frozen puffs to a parchment-lined baking sheet and bake at once, without thawing, allowing an additional 5 to 7 minutes baking time.

3. You can bake the curry puffs early in the day, bring them to room temperature, cover and refrigerate. Reheat them at 375 degrees F on a parchment-lined baking sheet in a single layer, uncovered, until heated through, 8 to 10 minutes.

DEVILED EGGS
with CILANTRO *and* CURRY

Makes 16 deviled eggs

I GREW UP ON DEVILED EGGS IN NORTH CAROLINA and still love to make, eat and serve them. A jolt of curry brings exotic flavor to my grandmother's recipe.

8 large eggs	½ teaspoon salt
3 tablespoons mayonnaise	¼ teaspoon freshly ground pepper
1 tablespoon curry powder, store-bought or homemade *(page 222, 224 or 226)*	1 large green onion, thinly sliced crosswise
½ teaspoon prepared mustard	2 tablespoons finely chopped fresh cilantro

Place the eggs in a medium saucepan with cold water to cover them, and bring to a rolling boil over high heat. Reduce the heat to medium-low, enough to keep the eggs at an active simmer, and cook for 9 minutes. Remove from the heat, drain and rinse in 2 changes of cold water. Add a dozen ice cubes to the water and leave the eggs to cool.

In a medium mixing bowl, combine the mayonnaise, curry powder, mustard, salt and pepper and stir well. Peel the eggs and cut in half lengthwise. Scoop out the yolks and add to the mixing bowl with the curry mayonnaise, and place the whites on a serving platter. Mash the yolks well with a fork to combine them with the mayonnaise. Work the mixture into a fairly smooth paste, scraping the bowl to combine everything well. Stir in the green onion and cilantro and mix well.

Using a table knife, stuff each egg white with a tablespoonful or so of the curried yolk mixture, dividing it evenly and rounding and smoothing the top of each egg as you work. Serve at once or cover and chill until shortly before serving time.

NOTE

⊛ These keep well for up to 2 days, covered and chilled.

SHRIMP SATAY *with* THAI-STYLE PEANUT SAUCE

Serves 4 to 6; makes 1⅓ cups sauce

THIS DISH ALONE has created a huge following for many a Thai restaurant and with good reason. Thai cooks adapted the Malay-style peanut sauce for their version of this Indonesian dish, making a simple red curry enriched with ground peanuts and giving it a sweet-sour punch with palm sugar and tamarind. The spicy peanut sauce is equally tasty with skewers of grilled vegetables or firm tofu and with any briefly marinated meat. Satay vendors in Thailand usually use thinly sliced pork and often include toasted bread along with the skewers of meat, lest any remaining sauce go to waste.

Satay makes a terrific yet simple party dish, especially if you prepare the peanut sauce in advance and delegate the grilling duties to one of your guests.

Red Curry Peanut Sauce

- 1 cup unsweetened coconut milk
- 1 tablespoon red curry paste, store-bought or homemade *(page 218)*
- ¾ cup chicken or vegetable broth
- 5 tablespoons peanut butter
- 2 tablespoons palm sugar *(page 253)* or light or dark brown sugar
- 1 tablespoon plus 1 teaspoon freshly squeezed lime juice or tamarind liquid *(page 238)*
- ½ teaspoon salt

Shrimp Satay

½ cup unsweetened coconut milk

1½ teaspoons curry powder,
   store-bought or homemade
   (page 222, 224 or 226)

1 teaspoon palm sugar or light
   or dark brown sugar

½ teaspoon salt

1 pound medium shrimp,
   peeled and deveined

Bamboo skewers for grilling

Sweet and Sour Cucumber
   Salad *(page 202)*

Make the Red Curry Peanut Sauce. In a medium saucepan, bring the coconut milk to a gentle boil over medium heat. Cook about 3 minutes, stirring often, until fragrant and slightly thickened. Add the curry paste and cook 3 minutes, mashing and stirring to dissolve the paste. Add the broth and peanut butter and bring to a gentle boil. Cook 4 to 5 minutes, stirring often, until the sauce is smooth, heated through and thickened. Stir in the sugar, lime juice or tamarind liquid and salt and cook 2 to 3 minutes more, until the sauce is smooth. Taste and adjust the seasonings for a pleasing balance of sweet, sour and salty flavors, adding more lime juice or tamarind liquid or salt as needed.

Remove from the heat, transfer to a bowl and bring to room temperature. The surface of the sauce may darken as it stands, so stir it well before serving. Serve at room temperature.

Make the Shrimp Satay. In a medium bowl, combine the coconut milk, curry powder, sugar and salt and stir well. Add the shrimp and toss to coat evenly with the marinade. Cover and refrigerate 30 minutes to 1 hour.

To cook the shrimp, preheat a grill or broiler until very hot. Thread 2 of the marinated shrimp onto each bamboo skewer, and place them on the hot grill or under the broiler 3 to 5 minutes, turning once, until the shrimp are pink, firm and cooked through. Serve hot or warm with the peanut sauce and Sweet and Sour Cucumber Salad.

◀◀◀◀ ▶▶▶▶

NOTES

⊛ You can use any Thai-style curry paste, though red, mussamun or yellow pastes will give the most appealing color to the sauce, since all of them are made with a base of dried red chilies.

⊛ If you make the sauce more than 30 minutes in advance, cover it and refrigerate until serving time. It thickens as it stands, so reheat it gently and thin it with a little chicken or vegetable broth to the consistency you like. You can keep the sauce covered and refrigerated for 2 days.

⊛ To keep the bamboo skewers from catching fire, use the Thai satay vendors' trick of placing the skewers on the grill so that the shrimp extend out over the heat source but the skewers do not. Or soak the skewers in cold water to cover for an hour or so before grilling.

⊛ Try this with chicken, marinating bite-size chunks of breast meat or dark meat for 30 minutes to 1 hour and then cooking over a hot grill until done.

Savory Curried Nuts

Makes 3 cups

So LITTLE EFFORT for such a yummy reward! If you love hot food, add a dash of cayenne. Use all almonds, all cashews, all pecans or any combination to total 3 cups of nuts. Pecans are especially divine, since they capture the seeds in their crannies. These keep well, although it is difficult to test that out since they disappear fast.

2 tablespoons vegetable oil	1 cup whole pecans
2 teaspoons cumin seeds	1 teaspoon curry powder,
2 teaspoons black or brown mustard seeds *(page 241)*	store-bought or homemade *(page 222, 224 or 226)*
1 cup whole raw almonds	1 tablespoon soy sauce
1 cup dry-roasted salted whole cashews	

Preheat the oven to 400 degrees F and place a large ungreased baking sheet by the stove.

In a large, heavy saucepan or Dutch oven, combine the oil, cumin seeds and mustard seeds and heat over medium heat until the seeds begin to pop, 1 to 2 minutes. Stir constantly for 1 more minute while the seeds continue to pop.

Add the nuts and curry powder and stir well. Cook 3 minutes, stirring constantly, to heat the nuts through. Add the soy sauce and stir well. Transfer to the baking sheet; spread out into a single layer. Roast the nuts for 10 minutes, until they are fragrant.

Remove from the oven and set aside to cool to room temperature, about 30 minutes. Transfer to a jar and seal airtight. Store at room temperature up to 2 weeks.

CHAPTER 2

SOUPS

SAY THE WORD "SOUP" to yourself and watch images float up like steam off a simmering stockpot: a cozy kitchen on a cold, cloudy day, a patient cook giving the pot a knowing stir, a table set simply with big spoons, crockery bowls, a hunk of butter and a crusty loaf of bread. Whether we order it in an elegant restaurant or open a can to heat up on the stove, soup has the peaceful power to comfort us as it turns hunger into satisfaction.

My dictionary defines soup as "liquid food," and since many traditional curries could also fit this definition, I made this chapter a collection of soups in the Western sense. Any of the following could be the centerpiece of a meal, paired with sandwiches or a salad. Several are hearty supper dishes, kissing-cousins of stew: Mulligatawny Soup, Spicy Peanut Chicken Soup West African-Style and Roasted Red Lentil Soup. The remaining recipes are for simple, creamy soups celebrating one vegetable or another, all in the embrace of incomparable curry flavors: Curried Kabocha Pumpkin Soup, Curried Cream of Mushroom Soup, Curried Chunky Potato Soup, Carrot-Ginger Soup and Cool Curry Cucumber and Tomato Soup.

ALTHOUGH THEY DO NOT demand complicated kitchen technique, they generally require your presence, with varying levels of attention, for an hour or more. If time is an issue, you could cook up a double batch or have two or three soups going at once. Ideally, you would be assisted by a friend or two to share the labor and provide company as you work.

You will then have abundant homemade soup to share, which can be devoured sooner as well as later, after its flavors have had the opportunity to blossom.

Except for Cool Curry Cucumber and Tomato Soup, each of these potages freezes wonderfully, allowing you to lay in a supply for a week or a month hence. Long after your cooking session is a memory, you will have a spice-infused supper simmering on your stove for those nights when you yearn for truly delicious yet truly fast food.

Soups

Mulligatawny Soup

Serves 10 to 12

THIS HEARTY OFFERING became popular during the era of the British Raj, when chefs and home cooks put an English spin on a simple southern Indian soup made with lentils and black pepper. Versions abound to this day. Make this one on a chilly afternoon when you are home for a few hours with time to chop up an armload of fresh vegetables and tend a simmering chicken. Your reward will be the sizzle and perfume of garlic and onions and a winter feast.

Soup Stock

1 whole chicken (3-4 pounds); *see Notes*

4 tart green apples, such as Granny Smiths, coarsely chopped, core and all

4 large carrots, peeled and coarsely chopped

4 celery stalks, coarsely chopped

2 medium onions, coarsely chopped, skin and all

1 garlic head, halved crosswise to expose cloves

5 bay leaves

1 2-inch hunk fresh ginger, coarsely chopped

2 tablespoons whole green peppercorns, black or white peppercorns, or 1 teaspoon freshly ground pepper

1 tablespoon fresh rosemary leaves or 2 tablespoons whole dried leaves or 1 teaspoon ground dried

1 teaspoon whole cardamom seeds or 1 teaspoon ground

Soup

4	tablespoons butter	1	tablespoon minced garlic
1	medium onion, finely chopped (about 1 cup)	2	tablespoons mild Indian curry paste or 1 tablespoon red curry paste, store-bought or homemade *(page 218)*
1	cup finely chopped carrots		
½	cup finely chopped celery	1½	teaspoons salt
½	cup raw rice	½	teaspoon freshly ground pepper, plus more at serving time
⅓	cup raw red lentils		
¼	cup flour	1	bunch fresh cilantro
1	teaspoon ground coriander		

Make the Soup Stock. Rinse the chicken well in cold water and place in a large stockpot with the remaining stock ingredients. Add cold water to cover and bring to a rolling boil over medium heat. Reduce the heat to maintain a simmer and cook about 1 hour, until the meat falls easily from the bones.

Strain the stock, reserving the liquid and chicken but discarding the vegetables. When the chicken is cool enough to handle, pick the meat from the bones. Tear large chunks into small pieces and set the meat aside, discarding the skin and bones.

If you are preparing the stock in advance, let the stock and meat cool to room temperature, cover and refrigerate separately for 1 day. A layer of fat will congeal on top when it is thoroughly chilled; skim it off and discard it.

Make the Soup. In a large saucepan or Dutch oven, melt the butter over medium heat. Add the onion, carrots and celery and cook 10 minutes, stirring often, until the vegetables are softened and fragrant. Add the rice and lentils and cook 2 minutes, stirring constantly.

Add the flour, coriander, garlic, curry paste and a splash of the soup stock. Cook 1 to 2 minutes, stirring often to soften and dissolve the curry paste and mix everything well. Slowly add the remaining soup stock (you should have about 8 cups), stirring constantly to maintain the smooth body of the soup. Add the chicken, salt and pepper and cook 10 minutes, stirring occasionally. Taste and add salt, if needed. Serve hot, with a sprinkling of finely chopped cilantro and freshly ground pepper on top of each bowl.

◀◀◀▶▶▶

NOTES

⊛ Look for a whole frying chicken, as these smaller birds are just the right size for this soup.

⊛ Whole herbs and spices are called for in the stock so that it will be clear after cooking. But use ground if you need to; they will work fine.

⊛ This soup tends to thicken as it stands. If it seems too thick after you have reheated it gently, use water or broth to thin it to the texture you like.

⊛ For a faster version, omit the recipe for Soup Stock. Substitute 8 cups canned chicken broth, preferably low-sodium, and about 2 cups cooked shredded chicken. Add bay leaves and a sprig of rosemary, if you have it on hand, to enhance the flavor of the canned broth. Taste before adding any salt and add only as needed.

⊛ Sealed airtight, this soup freezes well for up to 2 months.

SPICY PEANUT CHICKEN SOUP WEST AFRICAN-STYLE

Serves 6

HERE YOU HAVE A SPECTACULAR DISH to enjoy three different ways. Not only does it make a rich, satisfying bowl of soup, it shines as a velvety curry sauce served over rice and with steamed vegetables, or over a bowl of noodles. Use a hot curry powder and extra serrano chili peppers, if you like things on the spicy side.

1 pound boneless, skinless
   chicken breast

⅓ cup flour

2 tablespoons curry powder,
   store-bought or homemade
   (page 222, 224 or 226)

1 teaspoon salt

¼ teaspoon freshly ground green,
   white or black peppercorns

¼ cup vegetable oil

1 tablespoon minced fresh ginger

1 tablespoon minced garlic

1 serrano chili pepper, seeded
   and minced

5 cups chicken broth, *divided*

¼ cup peanut butter *(see Note)*

½ teaspoon ground coriander

½ teaspoon salt

4 green onions, finely chopped

6 tablespoons Cilantro Mint
   Chutney *(page 189)*, or
   3 tablespoons each finely
   chopped fresh cilantro
   and mint

1 lime, cut lengthwise into
   6 wedges

Rinse the chicken breast and pat dry with paper towels. Slice it crosswise into strips, about 2 inches long and ¼ inch thick. In a small, sturdy paper bag, combine the flour, curry powder, salt and pepper and shake well. Add the chicken pieces and shake to coat well. Transfer carefully to a plate and place by the stove.

In a medium saucepan, heat the oil over medium heat until a pinch of the flour mixture dropped into the oil sizzles at once, about 1 minute. Add the chicken pieces, sprinkling them in so that they do not clump together. Cook 4 minutes, tossing occasionally to cook the chicken evenly. Add the ginger, garlic, chili pepper and ½ cup of the broth to the saucepan and cook for 3 minutes, scraping the pan with a spatula and stirring to combine everything well.

Add the peanut butter, stirring quickly to incorporate it with the chicken. Add the remaining 4½ cups broth slowly, stirring continuously to maintain the even texture of the soup. Add the coriander, salt and green onions and stir well. Simmer 10 minutes, stirring occasionally, until the soup is fairly smooth, well combined and heated through.

To serve, pour the hot soup into individual serving bowls and top each with a tablespoon of Cilantro Mint Chutney or cilantro and mint and a generous squeeze of juice from a lime wedge. Serve at once.

◀◀◀▶▶▶▶

NOTE

 If you use pure peanut butter similar to the freshly ground types found in health food stores, add 2 teaspoons sugar along with the peanut butter. If you use commercial, processed peanut butter that contains sugar, you will not need to add sugar to the recipe.

CURRIED KABOCHA PUMPKIN SOUP

Serves 6 to 8

R ING IN COOL WEATHER with this autumnal soup, fortified with the flavor of cashews and sweetened with fruit chutney and golden winter squash. Kabocha pumpkin is the sweetest member of the hard squash family, with dense, orange flesh, a small, plump pumpkin shape and a bumpy variegated skin ranging from deep green to yellow and orange. You could substitute 3 cups of any cooked, mashed winter squash, including butternut, sweet dumpling or acorn. For a speedy version, use canned pumpkin puree and either milk or soy milk instead of cashew milk.

1 kabocha pumpkin (about 4 pounds)	3 cups dry-roasted salted cashews
6 tablespoons butter or vegetable oil	10 tablespoons Apple Raisin Chutney *(page 194)* or any fruit chutney
¾ cup coarsely chopped shallots	3 cups chicken or vegetable broth
2 teaspoons curry powder, store-bought or homemade *(page 222, 224 or 226)*	Salt to taste

To prepare the pumpkin, place it on a cutting board and cut it lengthwise into quarters. Cut off and discard the stem and end portions, and scrape out and discard the seeds and fibers from the center. Chop the pumpkin into large chunks, 3 to 5 inches long, leaving the skin on. Rinse the chunks well, place in a large, heavy saucepan or Dutch oven and add water to cover. Bring to a rolling boil over medium heat, reduce the heat to maintain an active simmer and cook until the pumpkin is tender, about 30 minutes.

Drain well, reserving the cooking liquid for the soup, and set the pumpkin chunks on a platter to cool. Combine the pumpkin cooking liquid with enough water to total 6 cups and set aside. Keep the saucepan or Dutch oven handy for finishing the soup.

When the pumpkin chunks are cool enough to handle, scoop out and reserve the pulp and set it aside, discarding the skin. You will have about 3 cups of mashed pumpkin.

In a small frying pan over medium heat, heat the butter or oil and add the shallots. Cook over medium heat, tossing often, until the shallots are shiny, fragrant and tender, about 5 minutes. Add the curry powder and cook, tossing, for 1 to 2 minutes, to toast it and combine it evenly with the shallots. Remove from the heat and set aside.

In a blender, combine the cashews and the 6 cups of pumpkin cooking liquid. Blend at high speed until you have a smooth, rich cashew milk, pulsing on and off and scraping down the sides as needed to grind the cashews well, about 2 minutes. Transfer to a pitcher or bowl and set aside.

In the blender, combine the cooked pumpkin, chutney and shallot mixture and blend until smooth, adding the cashew milk as needed to move the blades and grind well.

In the saucepan or Dutch oven in which the pumpkin was cooked, combine the pumpkin puree with the remaining cashew milk and the broth and bring to a gentle boil over medium heat, stirring often. Reduce the heat to maintain an active simmer and cook 10 minutes more. Serve hot or warm.

◀◀◀▶▶▶

NOTE

⊛ Like many creamy, pureed soups, this one thickens as it stands, so use water, broth or milk to thin it to the consistency you like once you have reheated it.

CURRIED CREAM *of* MUSHROOM SOUP

Serves 6 to 8

THIS RICH, VELVETY SOUP makes the most of the natural earthiness of curry spices and mushrooms. Set aside a little time for this one, as it needs slow, careful cooking to bring its satisfying flavors together. If you like, substitute half-and-half, whole milk or unflavored soy milk for the cashew milk or whipping cream. If shiitake mushrooms are difficult to find, use more ordinary mushrooms for a total of 2½ pounds.

6   tablespoons butter or vegetable oil

4   cups coarsely chopped onion

1   tablespoon fresh thyme or 1 teaspoon dried

2   pounds mushrooms, coarsely chopped

½   pound fresh shiitake mushrooms, or 10 dried, coarsely chopped *(see Notes)*

2   tablespoons chopped garlic

½   cup beer, apple cider or vegetable broth

4   teaspoons mild Indian-style curry paste or 2 teaspoons red curry paste, store-bought or homemade *(page 218)*

4   cups vegetable broth

1   cup cashew milk *(page 233)* or whipping cream

In a large, heavy saucepan or Dutch oven, heat the butter or oil over medium heat. Add the onion and thyme and cook 10 minutes, tossing occasionally, until the onion is softened and transparent. Add all the mushrooms and garlic and increase the heat to high. Cook, stirring often, until the mushrooms are steaming, about 10 minutes. Reduce the heat to medium-low and cook slowly, stirring occasionally, until the juices thicken and the onion begins to stick, about 25 minutes.

Add the beer, cider or broth and stir well, scraping to release the mushroom mixture from the bottom of the pan. Add the curry paste and cook 3 to 5 minutes, mashing and stirring often. Remove from the heat, carefully transfer the mushroom mixture to a blender and puree about 1 minute, until thick and smooth, scraping down the sides as needed.

Transfer the puree to a clean medium saucepan and add the broth. Place over medium heat and bring to a gentle boil, stirring almost constantly to prevent the soup from sticking or burning. Slowly whisk in the cashew milk or cream, bring to a simmer and remove from the heat. Serve hot.

◀◀◀▶▶▶

NOTES

❀ Dried shiitake mushrooms are available in the Asian food section of many supermarkets, in Asian grocery stores or by mail (pages 257 to 259). They are costly, but they pay their way in deep, extraordinary flavor. You can also use large dried Chinese mushrooms. (See page 254 and page 248 for more detail on shiitake mushrooms and dried Chinese mushrooms.) To use dried mushrooms in this recipe, soak them for 30 minutes in warm water to cover. Then drain well and coarsely chop, stems and all, and continue as directed.

❀ You can cover and refrigerate any leftover soup for up to 3 days, or seal airtight and freeze for about 1 month. Reheat leftover soup gently. This soup tends to thicken as it stands, so add a little broth or water as needed to thin it to the texture you like.

ROASTED RED LENTIL SOUP

Serves 8 to 10

YOU WILL LOVE this flame-colored, thick soup, earthy in texture and alive with spices. The salmon-pink lentils, called *masoor dal*, give color and body to this dish and are widely available in health-food stores. This soup needs an hour of simmering time, so make it on a day when you can wander in and out of the kitchen tending it. Then you can enjoy it as a quick, robust meal for days after.

Serve with Chapatis or Pooris (page 176 or 182) and a bright bowl of cucumbers, cherry tomatoes and bell peppers tossed with poppy seed dressing.

1 tablespoon curry powder, store-bought or homemade (*page 222, 224 or 226*)

1 teaspoon ground cumin

1 teaspoon asafetida (*see Note*)

1 teaspoon ground ginger

½ teaspoon freshly ground pepper

3 tablespoons vegetable oil

2 teaspoons black or brown mustard seeds (*page 241*)

2 teaspoons cumin seeds

¼ cup white sesame seeds

1 tablespoon finely chopped garlic

2 cups raw red lentils

1 cup finely chopped onion

2 cups finely chopped celery

2 cups finely chopped carrots

5 cups chicken or vegetable broth

3 cups water

1 cup canned diced tomatoes with juice

1 teaspoon salt

Combine the curry powder, cumin, asafetida, ginger and pepper in a small bowl, stir to mix well and set aside.

In a large soup pot or Dutch oven, heat the oil over medium heat for 1 minute. Add the mustard seeds and cumin seeds and stir almost constantly until the seeds pop, 1 to 2 minutes. Reduce the heat to low and add the sesame seeds. Cook, stirring, until the sesame seeds are golden brown, 1 to 2 minutes.

Add the garlic and the small bowl of spices and stir well for about 30 seconds to toast the spices. Add the lentils and cook 5 minutes, still over medium heat, stirring often. Add the onion, celery and carrots and cook, stirring, for about 1 minute. Add the broth and water, bring to a rolling boil and reduce the heat to maintain an active simmer. Cook for about 30 minutes, stirring occasionally, until the lentils are soft and easily mashed.

Add the tomatoes and continue cooking 25 minutes to mingle the flavors, stirring occasionally. Stir in the salt and taste, adding a little more salt, if needed. Serve hot or warm.

NOTE

⊛ Asafetida is a pungent seasoning powder used in traditional Indian cooking. Ground from the hardened amber-colored resin of a plant in the fennel family, it is available in Indian markets and by mail-order (pages 257 and 258). You can omit it if you prefer, and still have a marvelous soup. See Glossary (page 240) for more on asafetida.

CURRIED CHUNKY POTATO SOUP

Serves 8

I F YOU KEEP YOUR WINTER PANTRY stocked with potatoes, onions and garlic, you can have homemade soup for supper without a trip to the store. This recipe adds a bright curry touch to humble but satisfying potato soup, chunky with potatoes and fragrant with garlic. The soup comes together quickly, freeing you to tend to other tasks while it simmers away. For cooks who enjoy experimenting, here is a good place to omit the curry powder and play with appealing spice combinations.

2 tablespoons vegetable oil	¼ cup finely chopped garlic
4 medium onions, finely chopped	(about 1 dozen large cloves)
4 cups peeled red-skinned	8 cups chicken or vegetable broth
potatoes, chopped into	2 cups unsweetened coconut milk,
½-inch chunks	milk or soy milk
2 tablespoons curry powder,	½ teaspoon salt
store-bought or homemade	3 tablespoons minced fresh
(page 222, 224 or 226)	cilantro or parsley

Heat the oil in a large saucepan over medium heat until a bit of onion sizzles at once when added. Add the onions and cook 5 minutes, tossing often, until they are shiny, fragrant and transparent. Add the potatoes and cook, stirring frequently, until they are steaming, about 3 minutes. Reduce the heat to medium-low and add the curry powder and garlic. Cook about 3 minutes, tossing often, until the curry powder and garlic are fragrant and evenly mixed with the vegetables.

Increase the heat to medium, add the broth and bring to a boil. Reduce the heat to maintain a simmer and cook about 45 minutes, stirring occasionally, until the potatoes are tender. Add the milk and salt, stir well, and cook until heated through, about 5 minutes more. Taste and adjust the seasonings. Serve hot or warm, sprinkled with cilantro or parsley.

NOTE

⊛ You can use other types of potatoes, including white rose, Idaho and new potatoes.

CARROT-GINGER SOUP

Serves 4 to 6

ERE IS A BOWL OF WARM SUNSHINE, bright with carrot color and fresh ginger and sweet with red bell pepper and dates. You can chop the vegetables coarsely since the soup is pureed before you serve it.

4 tablespoons butter, ghee, store-bought or homemade *(page 234)*, or vegetable oil

1 cup coarsely chopped onion

½ cup coarsely chopped red bell pepper

1 tablespoon grated or minced fresh ginger

1 teaspoon curry powder, store-bought or homemade *(page 222, 224 or 226)*

1 pound carrots, trimmed, peeled and coarsely chopped (about 4 cups)

About 1 cup water

6 pitted dates

1 cup unsweetened coconut milk, milk or soy milk

½ teaspoon salt

2 tablespoons freshly squeezed lime juice

1 tablespoon finely chopped fresh mint or parsley

In a medium saucepan over medium heat, heat the butter, ghee or oil. Add the onion and red pepper and cook, tossing often, until they become soft and shiny and give up their juices, about 10 minutes. Add the ginger and curry powder and cook 2 minutes more. Add the carrots and 1 cup water, adding more water as needed to cover the carrots. Let it come to a boil, reduce the heat to maintain a gentle boil and cook, stirring occasionally, until the carrots are soft, about 30 minutes.

Strain out the vegetables, reserving their cooking liquid, and place them in a blender along with the dates. Puree, adding the reserved cooking liquid as needed to move the blades. Blend until you have a thick, smooth puree, stopping occasionally to scrape down the sides. Add the milk and blend until everything is well combined, adding additional cooking liquid as needed to achieve the consistency you like. Add the salt and lime juice; puree.

Return the soup to the pan and cook over medium heat, 3 to 5 minutes, until heated through. Taste and adjust the seasoning as needed. Serve hot or warm, sprinkled with fresh mint or parsley.

NOTE

⊛ Like many creamy, pureed soups, this tends to thicken as it stands. After reheating, use water, broth or milk to thin it to the consistency you like.

COOL CURRY CUCUMBER and TOMATO SOUP

Serves 4

THIS IS ACTUALLY A COMBINATION OF TWO SEPARATE SOUPS, poured into one bowl and swirled together lightly for a striking presentation. The flavors and colors of the tomato and cucumber purees remain distinct and counterpoint each other. Or you can stir the two together before serving and enjoy the fresh-as-salsa flavors in cool harmony.

Cold Tomato Soup	Cold Cucumber Soup
1 tablespoon olive oil	¼ cup coarsely chopped celery
1 cup finely chopped onion	3 green onions, coarsely chopped
1 teaspoon minced garlic	2 large cucumbers, peeled, seeded and chopped
1 teaspoon peeled, minced fresh ginger	1 serrano chili pepper, stemmed and chopped
1 teaspoon mild Indian-style curry paste or ½ teaspoon red curry paste, store-bought or homemade *(page 218)*	1 tablespoon chopped fresh mint
1 can (11½-ounce) V8 juice	1 tablespoon chopped fresh cilantro
	1 tablespoon seasoned rice vinegar or another white vinegar, mixed with ¼ teaspoon sugar
	½ teaspoon salt

Make the Cold Tomato Soup. In a medium frying pan, heat the oil over medium heat for about 1 minute and add the onion. Cook, tossing often, until it is shiny, fragrant and transparent, about 5 minutes. Add the garlic, ginger and curry paste and cook, tossing occasionally to mingle the flavors, about 3 minutes. Add the V8 juice and cook 5 minutes, stirring occasionally, until well combined and heated through.

Remove from the heat, transfer to a blender and puree for about 1 minute, until smooth. Transfer to a pitcher or bowl, cool to room temperature, cover and chill.

Make the Cold Cucumber Soup. Combine all the ingredients, except the salt, in a blender and blend at high speed for 1 to 2 minutes until smooth, stopping occasionally to scrape down the sides. Add the salt and taste, adding a little more salt if needed. Transfer to a pitcher or bowl, cover and chill until serving time.

To serve, use two small pitchers to pour equal amounts of each soup into opposite sides of a serving bowl. Swirl once with a spoon to patch the colors together and serve cold.

NOTES

⊛ For a simple summer soup when a striking presentation is not the goal, combine the cooled tomato soup with the cucumber soup in a large bowl and whisk to combine well. Cover and chill.

⊛ If you have fresh-from-the-garden pickling cucumbers or the soft-skinned hothouse or Japanese varieties, there is no need to seed or peel them. If you use the large, dark-green waxy cucumbers commonly found in supermarkets, you will need to peel and seed them as directed.

⊛ Seasoned rice vinegar contains sugar, so if you use another kind of white vinegar, you should add about ¼ teaspoon sugar.

CHAPTER 3

SALADS AND DRESSINGS

CURRY FLAVORS SUIT SALAD beautifully, adding a sizzle of heat and a sparkle of spice to this coolest of courses. Here you will find a toss-up of wonderful possibilities, from homey coleslaw and perfect pasta to snazzy shrimp and lentil salad jazzed up with a delectable curry vinaigrette.

Use curry seasonings to brighten some of your favorite recipes. Curried Cashew Chicken Salad and Curried Tuna Salad with Red Grapes and Toasted Almonds provide uptown versions of these old friends, dressy enough for company yet simple to make. Curried Egg Salad is fantastic as a snack on crackers or as a sandwich on toasted whole-wheat bread. Curried Barbecued Chicken Salad with Rainbow Coleslaw and Crispy Wonton Ribbons is irresistible, and while it takes some time to put together, you can do it in stages and use it on a summer evening as a one-dish meal. Shrimp and Sweet Corn Salad with Curried Avocado Aioli is another winner, hearty enough to anchor your menu and yet fine as a colorful addition to a buffet.

You can use these salads to cool off a red-hot curry menu or to add a touch of spice to a mainstream meal.

Salads *and* Dressings

CURRIED TUNA SALAD *with* RED GRAPES *and* TOASTED ALMONDS

Serves 8

TURN THAT FAMILIAR CAN OF TUNA into a star attraction in this appealing salad. Most of the ingredients come from your everyday pantry, and if you want to serve it without running out to buy red grapes, substitute a cup of raisins or a little chopped apple for a sweet, contrasting note of fruit.

This salad is terrific stuffed into a pita pocket with a handful of baby spinach leaves or shredded romaine. It is also special enough to serve on a bed of lettuce or stuffed into sweet red pepper cups as a luncheon course.

½ cup sliced almonds

2 cans (each 6-ounce) water-packed albacore tuna

½ cup mayonnaise

2 teaspoons curry powder, store-bought or homemade *(page 222, 224 or 226)*

2 tablespoons freshly squeezed lemon juice

3 tablespoons chopped fresh parsley

½ teaspoon salt

¼ teaspoon freshly ground pepper

2 cups red grapes

Toast the almonds by placing them in a small, dry frying pan over medium heat. Cook 7 to 9 minutes, stirring and tossing often to toast them evenly and avoid burning them. Remove from the heat and transfer to a plate to cool to room temperature.

Drain the tuna and spoon it into a medium bowl. Add the mayonnaise, curry powder, lemon juice, parsley, salt and pepper and stir well, breaking any large chunks of tuna into smaller pieces.

Slice the grapes in half lengthwise, remove seeds if necessary, and add the grapes to the salad, stirring to combine everything well. Cover and chill until shortly before serving time.

Add the toasted almonds just before serving, sprinkling them on top of the salad or on individual portions, or stirring them into the salad just before using it to make sandwiches.

NOTES

⊗ To preserve their toasty flavor and crunch, it is best to add the almonds just before serving. You can keep cooled toasted almonds sealed airtight for several days at room temperature, although toasting them close to serving time will give the best flavor.

⊗ Red grapes have great visual appeal, but green grapes will taste wonderful as well.

NEW POTATO SALAD
with CURRY *and* PEAS

Serves 6 to 8

CURRY ADDS A LITTLE SIZZLE to this old favorite, so take it along to your next picnic or potluck. The salad keeps well and complements anything you grill. If new potatoes are difficult to find, use small white rose or any red-skinned potato instead and quarter them before cooking. If you can find fresh chives, snip them instead of green onions over the potatoes.

3   pounds new potatoes

2   teaspoons salt, *divided*

1   box (10-ounce) frozen peas, thawed (about 1½ cups)

½   cup mayonnaise

½   cup sour cream

1   teaspoon minced garlic

2   teaspoons curry powder, store-bought or homemade (*page 222, 224 or 226*)

1   teaspoon ground cumin

2   tablespoons red wine vinegar

1   teaspoon Worcestershire sauce

¼   teaspoon freshly ground pepper

3   green onions, thinly sliced crosswise

Scrub the potatoes but do not peel them. Put them in a large pot and add cold water to cover by 1 inch. Bring the water to a rolling boil and add 1 teaspoon of the salt. Cook until the potatoes are tender, about 15 minutes. Drain the potatoes and cool to room temperature. Chop them into large, bite-size pieces, place them in a large bowl and add the peas.

In a small bowl, combine the mayonnaise, sour cream, garlic, curry powder, cumin, vinegar, Worcestershire sauce, the remaining 1 teaspoon salt and pepper. Whisk together until smooth. Pour over the potatoes and peas, add the green onions, and toss gently to combine everything well. Cover and chill until shortly before serving time.

FRESH SPINACH SALAD
with CHUTNEY DRESSING

Serves 6

T HIS DRESSING IS TINGED with the sweetness of chutney and has a little curry kick. Toss it with any of the washed and prepared salad greens mixtures available in supermarkets whenever you need a change from the spinach called for here.

Dressing

¼ cup balsamic vinegar or
   red wine vinegar

½ cup homemade fruit chutney
   (see Notes) or store-bought
   mango chutney

1 tablespoon sugar

2 teaspoons minced garlic

2 teaspoons curry powder,
   store-bought or homemade
   (page 222, 224 or 226)

¼ teaspoon salt

⅓ cup olive oil

Salad

½ pound bacon

8 cups fresh spinach leaves

½ pound mushrooms,
   thinly sliced

1 cup fresh bean sprouts

Make the Dressing. In a blender or food processor fitted with the metal blade, combine the vinegar, chutney, sugar, garlic, curry powder and salt, and pulse to mix well. Add the oil and puree until smooth, 30 seconds to 1 minute. Cover and refrigerate until serving time.

Make the Salad. In a large frying pan, cook the bacon over medium-high heat until crisp. Transfer to paper towels to drain. When the bacon is cool enough to handle, crumble it, place in a small bowl and set aside. In a large salad bowl, combine the spinach, mushrooms and bean sprouts.

Add about half of the dressing and toss well. Add more dressing, if needed to coat the salad, and set aside the rest of the dressing in the refrigerator for another use. Sprinkle with the bacon and serve at once.

◀◀◀▶▶▶

NOTES

❁ You can use Fresh Mango Chutney (page 196), Apple Raisin Chutney (page 194), Ginger Pear Chutney (page 191) or Fresh Fig Chutney (page 190).

❁ The dressing will keep 2 to 3 days in the refrigerator, sealed airtight. Stir well before using.

CURRIED BROCCOLI SLAW *with* BACON *and* CASHEWS

Serves 6 to 8

TAKE A BREAK FROM COLESLAW with this cool, crunchy salad. Use the head or crown of a large broccoli stalk, or buy broccoli florets if you are short on time. Plan to make this in advance, as it tastes best after it has chilled for at least 2 hours. If you do not have a food processor, chop the broccoli by hand.

1½ pounds broccoli crowns	3 tablespoons sugar
½ cup finely chopped red onion	3 tablespoons cider vinegar
½ cup dark raisins	1 tablespoon curry powder,
½ cup chopped dry-roasted	store-bought or homemade
salted cashews	*(page 222, 224 or 226)*
½ cup mayonnaise	½ teaspoon salt
½ cup sour cream	6 slices bacon, cooked
	and crumbled

Cut the broccoli into 1-inch pieces. Place half the broccoli in a food processor. Pulse to finely chop the broccoli, but do not puree it. Transfer to a large bowl and repeat with the remaining broccoli, adding it to the bowl as well. You should have about 6 cups finely chopped broccoli.

Add the onion, raisins and cashews to the broccoli and toss to mix well.

In a small bowl, combine the mayonnaise, sour cream, sugar, vinegar, curry powder and salt and stir well. Pour this dressing over the broccoli and toss to coat everything well. Cover tightly and refrigerate for at least 2 hours. Just before serving, sprinkle the bacon on top and serve cold.

NOTE

 You can make this salad 24 hours in advance, keeping it airtight in the refrigerator until serving time.

LENTIL SALAD
with CURRY VINAIGRETTE

Serves 6 to 8

THIS IS A TASTY DELI-STYLE SALAD to keep on hand and pull out of the refrigerator whenever an ordinary supper needs a lift. Serve with rounds of cucumber and halved cherry tomatoes or a mound of shredded lettuce. The vinaigrette recipe makes enough to dress the lentils and still have some left for several more salads.

2 tablespoons olive oil	1 teaspoon salt
½ cup finely chopped celery	¼ teaspoon freshly ground pepper
½ cup finely chopped carrot	2 green onions, thinly sliced
½ cup finely chopped onion	crosswise
1 tablespoon minced garlic	2 tablespoons finely chopped
1 tablespoon peeled, minced	fresh cilantro or parsley
fresh ginger	About ¼ cup Curry Vinaigrette
1 cup raw brown lentils	*(page 86)*
1 bay leaf	
2 cups water	

In a medium frying pan with a tight-fitting lid, heat the oil over medium-high heat for about 30 seconds, until a bit of garlic sizzles as soon as it is dropped into the pan. Add the celery, carrot, onion, garlic and ginger and cook, tossing often, until the vegetables are tender and fragrant but not browned, about 5 minutes.

Reduce the heat to medium, add the lentils and stir well. Add the bay leaf, water, salt and pepper and bring to a gentle boil. Reduce the heat to maintain an active simmer, cover and cook about 1 hour, stirring occasionally, until the lentils are tender but still whole and most of the liquid is absorbed.

Drain the lentils if necessary and set aside to cool for about 15 minutes, discarding the bay leaf. While the lentils are still warm, toss with enough Curry Vinaigrette to moisten and season them. Add the green onions and cilantro or parsley and toss well. Serve at room temperature or chilled. Cover and refrigerate for up to 5 days.

S**HRIMP** *and* S**WEET** C**ORN** S**ALAD** *with* C**URRIED** A**VOCADO** A**IOLI**

Serves 4

T**HIS GORGEOUS SALAD** brings sweet and spicy flavors together in each colorful bite. Aioli is a classic mayonnaise heady with garlic, here enhanced with avocado for a smooth, luxurious texture that makes a perfect foil for the sweet yellow corn, black beans and tender pink shrimp. Fresh corn is ideal, but frozen, thawed kernels will work well in its place. Serve this salad on a bed of bibb lettuce, or mounded on a papaya or avocado half.

Chili garlic sauce is a delicious condiment available in Asian markets (see page 243), but you can substitute a few drops of Tabasco sauce if it is difficult to find.

2 tablespoons olive oil
   or other vegetable oil
½ cup finely chopped red onion
1 teaspoon minced garlic
1 teaspoon chili garlic sauce
   or several dashes of
   Tabasco sauce
2 medium red bell peppers, finely
   chopped (about 2 cups)
1 cup cooked corn kernels from
   2-3 ears of corn or 1 cup
   frozen corn, thawed

1 pound cooked medium shrimp
1 can (15-ounce) black beans,
   rinsed and drained
2 tablespoons freshly squeezed
   lemon juice
¼ cup finely chopped fresh
   cilantro
Bibb lettuce leaves
Curried Avocado Aioli
(page 87)

In a large frying pan over medium-high heat, heat the oil for about 30 seconds, until a bit of garlic dropped into the pan sizzles at once. Add the onion, garlic and chili garlic sauce or Tabasco sauce and cook, tossing, for about 1 minute until the onion is shiny and fragrant. Add the red peppers and cook until softened but not browned, tossing often, about 2 minutes. Add the corn, shrimp and beans and cook 1 to 2 minutes, tossing occasionally, until heated through.

Remove from the heat, and add the lemon juice and cilantro; toss well. Let stand 10 minutes and serve warm, or cool to room temperature, cover and chill. To serve, line 4 individual serving plates with lettuce leaves and divide the salad among them. Top each portion with a dollop of Curried Avocado Aioli and serve.

NOTES

⊛ If you want to serve this salad in a papaya or avocado half, cut the papaya or avocado in half lengthwise and discard the seeds or pit. Scoop out a little of the flesh from the inside, and slice off a thin, silver dollar-size section from the outside of the fruit so it will sit flat without rocking when you fill it and serve it.

⊛ You could also place a small bowl of Curried Avocado Aioli on a platter, line the remainder of the platter with bibb lettuce leaves, mound the shrimp salad on top of the lettuce and serve. Guests help themselves to salad and dollop the dressing on top of their portions.

⊛ If you have salad left over, you could toss it with the remaining dressing for a more casual presentation. Covered and chilled, the salad and dressing will keep 2 to 3 days.

CORONATION CHICKEN SALAD
with PINEAPPLE *and* WILD RICE

Serves 6 to 8

CREATED IN THE 1950S BY ROYAL CHEFS in celebration of the coronation of Queen Elizabeth II, this substantial main-course salad marries chicken, rice and pineapple in a tasty curry dressing flavored with yogurt and fresh ginger. My updated version uses wild rice along with white rice. You can use canned pineapple, but if you are looking for a spectacular presentation, use fresh and serve the salad in a hollowed-out pineapple shell.

½ cup dark raisins

3 tablespoons warm sherry or apple juice

2 teaspoons salt, *divided*

1 cup raw wild rice

1 cup raw jasmine rice or other long-grain white rice

1½ cups coarsely chopped fresh ripe pineapple (about ½ small pineapple)

1 small red bell pepper, seeded and coarsely chopped (about 1 cup)

2 cups coarsely chopped cooked chicken

5 green onions, thinly sliced crosswise

Curried Yogurt Dressing *(page 88)*

In a small bowl, combine the raisins with the sherry or apple juice and set aside to soak.

In a large cooking pot or Dutch oven, bring 6 cups water to a rolling boil over medium-high heat and add 1½ teaspoons of the salt. Add the wild rice and cook until it is tender and splits open to reveal its white core, about 50 minutes. Drain the rice well and set aside to cool to room temperature.

While the wild rice is cooking, combine the white rice with 1½ cups cold water and the remaining ½ teaspoon salt in a medium saucepan with a tight-fitting lid. Bring to a boil over medium-high heat and stir well. Reduce the heat to low, cover and cook 20 minutes undisturbed. Remove from the heat and let it stand 10 minutes. Uncover and fluff gently with a fork; set aside to cool to room temperature.

When both batches of rice have cooled, combine them in a large bowl with the raisins and their soaking liquid, the pineapple, red pepper and chicken. Add most of the green onions, reserving a handful for garnish, and toss well. Add the Curried Yogurt Dressing and toss again.

Cover and chill until shortly before serving time. Sprinkle with the remaining green onions and serve cold or cool.

◄◄◄►►►

NOTE

❀ Covered and chilled, this salad will keep 3 to 4 days.

WARM PASTA SALAD *with* SMOKED CHICKEN *in* CURRIED CHERRY TOMATO DRESSING

Serves 8 to 10

THE SWEET, TANGY TOMATO DRESSING in this salad marries well with the subtle spiciness of the curry and the smoky bite of the chicken. Use corkscrew pastas, such as fusilli or rotelle, or another short dried pasta, such as penne, orecchiette or ziti.

½ cup pine nuts	2 cups frozen peas (do not thaw)
1½ teaspoons salt, plus more if needed	2 cups coarsely chopped smoked chicken or smoked turkey
8 ounces dried corkscrew pasta or penne	1 red bell pepper, seeded and coarsely chopped
1 bag (10-ounce) cleaned fresh spinach leaves	Curried Cherry Tomato Dressing *(page 89)*

Toast the pine nuts in a small, dry frying pan over medium heat for 4 to 6 minutes, tossing often to prevent burning, until golden and fragrant. Transfer to a small plate and set aside to cool.

Bring a large pot of water to a rolling boil over high heat and add the salt. Add the pasta and cook about 10 minutes, until tender but still firm to the bite. Drain the pasta well and return it to the empty cooking pot. Immediately add the spinach, peas, chicken or turkey, red pepper and about ½ cup warm Curried Cherry Tomato Dressing. Toss well. Add the pine nuts and enough additional dressing to season and coat the ingredients, tossing to combine well. Taste and add a little salt, if needed.

Transfer to a large serving bowl and serve at once. Or let the salad cool, cover and chill up to 3 days. Serve warm, cool or at room temperature.

NOTE

⊗ If the spinach leaves are large, tear them into 3-inch pieces.

CURRIED CASHEW CHICKEN SALAD

Serves 4

WITH THE CRUNCH OF CASHEWS, the spiciness of curry and chutney and the sweetness of dried cherries, this dish will entice you to make it more than once. Chicken salad is the classic solution to leftover chicken, but you may find yourself cooking up one on Sunday night just to have this salad on hand for the week.

Enjoy the salad mounded on a bed of crisp greens, stuffed into a tomato shell for an elegant luncheon or into a pita pocket with romaine lettuce, or mounded on toasted raisin bread for a tea party.

Salad

2½ cups shredded cooked chicken

½ cup dry-roasted salted cashews

¼ cup dried cherries, dried cranberries or dark raisins

2 green onions, finely chopped

Dressing

½ cup mayonnaise

2 teaspoons sherry vinegar, raspberry vinegar or red wine vinegar

2 tablespoons store-bought mango chutney or homemade fruit chutney *(see Notes)*

1 teaspoon Dijon mustard

2 teaspoons curry powder, store-bought or homemade *(page 222, 224 or 226)*

¼ teaspoon freshly ground pepper

Make the Salad. In a large bowl, toss together the chicken, cashews, dried fruit and green onions.

Make the Dressing. In a separate small bowl, combine all the ingredients. Stir until the dressing is well combined and fairly smooth.

Add the dressing to the salad bowl and toss well until the chicken mixture is evenly coated with the dressing. Cover and chill until shortly before serving time.

◀◀◀ ▶▶▶

NOTES

⊛ If you need to cook chicken to make this salad, poach about 2½ pounds bone-in chicken breast with ribs attached. Remove from the broth, cool to room temperature, remove and discard the skin and bones, and tear the meat into shreds about 2 inches long. You could also poach about 1 pound boneless, skinless chicken breast, keeping in mind that it will cook more quickly and have less flavor.

⊛ I like the texture of hand-shredded chicken, but you can also use a knife to dice cooked chicken into medium cubes, if you prefer.

⊛ You can use any prepared sweet fruit chutney, or your own home-made, such as Fresh Mango Chutney (page 196), Ginger Pear Chutney (page 191), Apple Raisin Chutney (page 194) or Fresh Fig Chutney (page 190). If you use store-bought mango chutney, note that it may contain large, delicious chunks of preserved fruit. To be sure your salad has lots of mango flavor, remove a large piece or two of the fruit and finely chop it. Then mix the chopped mango back into the chutney, stir well and measure out 2 tablespoons of chutney for use in the recipe.

CURRIED BARBECUED CHICKEN SALAD *with* RAINBOW COLESLAW *and* CRISPY WONTON RIBBONS

Serves 6 to 8; makes about 1½ cups barbecue sauce

THIS SCRUMPTIOUS DISH is a cross between Chinese Chicken Salad and down-home Southern barbecue. The Curried Barbecue Sauce is terrific, so you may want to make more chicken than you need for the salad or try the sauce on ribs. Assembling the ingredients takes some time, but the results are both rewarding and healthful, and the salad is hearty enough to serve as a one-dish meal.

If you are in a hurry, you can substitute canned crispy chow mein noodles for the fried wonton ribbons, a bag of washed and prepared salad greens for the chopped lettuce and cabbage and roast chicken from the deli for the barbecued chicken breasts.

Curried Barbecue Sauce

½ cup soy sauce

½ cup ketchup

¼ cup balsamic vinegar

¼ cup honey

2 tablespoons curry powder, store-bought or homemade *(page 222, 224 or 226)*

2 tablespoons honey mustard or Dijon mustard

2 tablespoons peeled, minced fresh ginger

2 teaspoons minced garlic

1 teaspoon celery seeds

½ teaspoon freshly ground pepper

Chicken Salad

2 pounds boneless, skinless
   chicken breasts

3 tablespoons sherry vinegar,
   raspberry vinegar or
   red wine vinegar

1 tablespoon balsamic vinegar

½ cup vegetable oil

½ pound napa cabbage, shredded

¼ pound red cabbage, shredded

½ small head iceberg lettuce
   (about 6 ounces), shredded

¾ cup thinly sliced red onion,
   sliced lengthwise

1 cup grated or shredded carrots

½ cup chopped fresh cilantro

Wonton Ribbons

Vegetable oil for frying

25 wonton wrappers, sliced into
    ¼-inch-wide ribbons

Salt to taste

Make the Curried Barbecue Sauce. Combine the ingredients in a deep, medium bowl and whisk until smooth and well combined. Remove 4 tablespoons and set aside in a small bowl.

Make the Chicken Salad. Rinse the chicken breasts, pat dry with paper towels and place them in the Curried Barbecue Sauce. Turn the chicken in the sauce to coat evenly. Cover and refrigerate for 30 to 60 minutes.

In a small bowl, whisk together the vinegars, the oil and the reserved 4 tablespoons barbecue sauce until smooth and well combined. Set aside.

In a large salad bowl, combine the shredded cabbages, lettuce, onion, carrots and cilantro. Toss well, cover and chill until serving time.

To cook the chicken, remove it from the refrigerator and allow about 30 minutes for it to come to room temperature.

Meanwhile, preheat the grill or broiler until very hot. Grill or broil the chicken breasts for 5 to 6 minutes on each side, basting once or twice with the marinade, until the chicken is firm and the barbecue sauce is lightly caramelized. Transfer to a platter and cool for about 5 minutes. Place on a cutting board and slice crosswise into ½-inch-wide strips.

Make the Wonton Ribbons. Place a slotted spoon and a baking sheet lined with paper towels next to the stove for draining the wonton ribbons after frying. Pour the vegetable oil into a medium frying pan to a depth of 3 inches. Heat over medium-high heat for several minutes, until a bit of wonton wrapper dropped into the oil sizzles and puffs up at once. Carefully add a handful of wonton ribbons to the pan, sprinkling them over the surface of the oil. Cook about 1 minute, using the slotted spoon to separate them and cook them evenly.

When the wonton ribbons are crisp and golden brown, transfer to the paper-towel-lined baking sheet to drain. Cook the remaining wonton wrappers in batches the same way. Transfer the drained, cooked ribbons to a plate, sprinkle lightly with salt and set aside.

Assemble the salad. Place the chicken strips on the shredded greens. Stir the dressing, add it to the salad and toss well. Garnish with the wonton ribbons and serve at once.

NOTES

⊕ If you prepare each component of this salad in advance and set them aside, covering and chilling the chicken and vegetables, you can assemble it quickly whenever you are ready to serve it.

⊕ You can prepare the wonton ribbons up to 1 day in advance, sealing them airtight and storing them at room temperature.

C U R R I E D E G G S A L A D

Makes about 8 sandwiches

SMOOTH AND CREAMY, this flavorful egg salad is mildly spiced with curry. Spread it on whole-wheat bread for hearty picnic sandwiches or on thinly sliced white bread with the crusts removed for tasty tea sandwiches. Grating the onion as directed gives the salad a mild flavor without the wallop of raw chunks, but finely chopped onion will work.

8 hard-boiled eggs, finely chopped	½ teaspoon dry mustard
⅓ cup mayonnaise	½ teaspoon salt
1 teaspoon freshly squeezed lemon juice	¼ teaspoon freshly ground pepper
2 teaspoons curry powder, store-bought or homemade *(page 222, 224 or 226)*	3 drops Tabasco sauce
	1 small onion
	2 tablespoons minced fresh parsley
½ teaspoon sugar	

In a large bowl, combine the chopped hard-boiled eggs with the mayonnaise, lemon juice, curry powder, sugar, mustard, salt, pepper and Tabasco sauce. Stir well.

Cut the onion in half lengthwise and cut off the top, leaving the root end intact. Peel off the papery outer layers. Grate the onion by hand on the small holes of a box grater until you have about 2 tablespoons fine, moist onion puree. Add it to the egg salad along with the parsley and stir well.

Cover and chill until shortly before serving time.

CURRY VINAIGRETTE

Makes about ¾ cup

½ cup extra-virgin olive oil

¼ cup red wine vinegar

2 tablespoons minced shallots

1 jalapeño chili pepper,
   seeded and minced
   (about 1 tablespoon)

1 teaspoon minced garlic

1 tablespoon curry powder,
   store-bought or homemade
   (page 222, 224 or 226), or
   mild Indian-style curry paste

1 tablespoon light or dark
   brown sugar

½ teaspoon salt

¼ teaspoon freshly ground pepper

In a small bowl, combine all the ingredients and whisk until fairly smooth and well combined. Transfer to a jar and seal airtight. Refrigerate up to 2 weeks. Use chilled or at room temperature.

CURRIED AVOCADO AIOLI

Makes about 1¾ cups

THIS EXPRESS-LANE VERSION OF AIOLI uses a food processor or blender and pre-pared mayonnaise instead of homemade. For the best color and taste, choose Hass avocados, the pear-shaped, dark green ones with distinctive bumpy skin.

1 ripe avocado, preferably
   Hass variety

1 teaspoon minced garlic

¼ teaspoon garam masala,
   store-bought or homemade
   (page 228 or 230); optional

2 teaspoons curry powder,
   store-bought or homemade
   (page 222, 224 or 226)

1 cup mayonnaise

1 teaspoon honey

2 tablespoons freshly squeezed
   lime or lemon juice

Peel and pit the avocado, chop it coarsely and set aside. In a food processor or blender, combine the avocado, garlic, garam masala (if using) and curry powder and process until smooth, about 1 minute, stopping occasionally to scrape down the sides. Add the mayonnaise and honey and process until thick, smooth and well combined, about 1 minute.

Transfer to a small bowl, add the lime or lemon juice and stir well. To help maintain the avocado's green color, press plastic wrap directly onto the surface and cover tightly. Chill until shortly before serving time and serve cold or cool.

CURRIED YOGURT DRESSING

Makes about 1 cup

⅔ cup mayonnaise

½ cup plain yogurt

2 tablespoons raspberry vinegar
or red wine vinegar

1 tablespoon honey

1 tablespoon curry powder,
store-bought or homemade
(page 222, 224 or 226)

1 teaspoon Worcestershire sauce

1 teaspoon peeled, minced
fresh ginger

½ teaspoon minced garlic

Combine all the ingredients in a small bowl and whisk together until fairly smooth and well combined. Cover and chill until needed.

CURRIED CHERRY TOMATO DRESSING

Makes about 1 cup

2 pints cherry tomatoes or 1 can (28-ounce) diced tomatoes, drained well

½ cup plus 2 tablespoons olive oil, *divided*

¼ cup finely chopped shallots

¼ cup grated or shredded carrots

2 tablespoons peeled, minced fresh ginger

1 tablespoon minced garlic

1 tablespoon mild Indian-style curry paste, curry powder or 1½ teaspoons red curry paste, store-bought or homemade *(page 222, 224, 226 or 218)*

1 tablespoon light or dark brown sugar

¼ cup red wine vinegar

¼ teaspoon salt

Stem the cherry tomatoes and cut them into quarters, or drain the canned, diced tomatoes. Set aside.

In a large frying pan over medium-high heat, heat 2 tablespoons of the oil for about 30 seconds and add the shallots, carrots, ginger, garlic and curry paste or powder. Cook 3 to 4 minutes, tossing often, until the vegetables are shiny and tender. Add the tomatoes and brown sugar and continue cooking until the tomatoes soften and the dressing is bubbly, about 3 minutes. Reduce the heat to low and add the remaining ½ cup oil, the vinegar and the salt. Cook, stirring, until the dressing is heated through, about 1 minute. Remove from the heat, transfer to a small bowl and use as directed.

CHAPTER 4

MAIN COURSES

WITH A PARADE OF ROBUST dishes replete with curry spices and herbs, this chapter is the heart of the book. Here you will find the Thai specialties that were my irresistible invitation to the world of curry herbs and spices during my Peace Corps days in Thailand. You will also find Indian-style curries, Chinese-style curry stir-fries and my untraditional North American adaptations.

Three main theories exist regarding the origins of the word "curry," two linking it to India's southern region. In the Tamil language of southern India, *kari* refers to a dish with an abundance of sauce. *Kari* also is the word for a fresh herb beloved in southern India's kitchens. A third theory holds that the word curry derives from *kadhai*, a deep bowl-like cooking vessel that is standard equipment in a traditional Indian kitchen. How any one or a combination of these terms evolved into that universally pleasing word is unclear— and insignificant in the context of cooking curries.

What is clear, however, is that curry has traveled the world. When you want a classic international curry with plenty of sauce, try Pork Vindaloo Goa-Style, Malay-Style Rice Noodles with Shrimp in Coconut Curry Soup or Thai Mussamun Curry with Chicken, Potatoes and Peanuts. For curry-flavored classics without sauce, cook Tandoori Chicken Homestyle, which lets you enjoy the dish without installing a huge clay oven next to your stove. Singapore Curry Noodles with Green Peppers and Shrimp is one of my favorite items at Chinese dim-sum restaurants; my version uses the wire-thin rice noodles widely available in supermarkets. Selections from North America include Curried Scallops in Parchment Packages and Pork Chops with Curried Chutney Sauce.

 HETHER YOUR CURRIES start with homemade or store-bought powders and pastes, remember that, like wine and people, most of these dishes improve with age. Many, particularly those with an abundance of sauce, will continue to develop in flavor after they have cooled. When possible, make your curry in advance, cool it, cover and chill for several hours or overnight. Then reheat it gently at serving time and enjoy the complexity at its zenith.

Traditional Southeast Asian-style curries made with coconut milk tend to release oil as they cook. The appearance of tiny orange pools glistening on top of curry is the sign of a properly made dish. If you prefer, however, you can skim off the oil as your curry cooks, or make it ahead, cool, chill it well, and scoop out and discard the bright orange chunks of fat. Coconut curries also tend to separate if they stand a while, as coconut milk does. Simply stir well and reheat gently to bring everything back together.

If you have access to fresh herbs, such as lemongrass, galanga, ginger and wild lime leaves, you can boost the flavors of a quick curry without making a paste from scratch. Simply cut any or all of these herbs into large, thin slices and toss a handful into the simmering sauce. Then remove these herbs before you serve.

Intense by their nature, curry flavors call out for company—whether a platter of plain rice, a pile of noodles or a stack of flatbreads warm from the griddle. Check Rice and Bread (page 160) for an array of supporting players for your all-star curry dishes.

Main Courses

CHICKEN CURRY

Serves 4 to 6

THIS CLASSIC CURRY makes a centerpiece for a special occasion and needs only a crisp green salad, a bowl of chutney and a generous pot of basmati or jasmine rice to round out the meal. You will have lots of luxurious sauce surrounding the tender chicken pieces. This curry improves as it stands, so make it a day ahead. Add the raisins, cashews and green onions when you reheat it at serving time.

4 tablespoons butter or ghee, store-bought or homemade *(page 234)*

2 medium onions, thinly sliced

1 teaspoon peeled, minced fresh ginger

1 teaspoon minced garlic

3 pounds chicken, cut into small serving pieces *(see Notes)*

1 tablespoon curry powder, store-bought or homemade *(page 222, 224 or 226)*

½ teaspoon ground cumin

½ teaspoon ground coriander

1 teaspoon salt

½ teaspoon freshly ground pepper

⅔ cup plain yogurt

2 tablespoons freshly squeezed lemon juice

½ cup dark raisins

½ cup dry-roasted salted cashews

3 green onions, thinly sliced crosswise

In a large frying pan with a tight-fitting lid, heat the butter or ghee over medium-high heat until melted and bubbly. Add the onions and cook, uncovered, until softened, about 4 minutes. Add the ginger and garlic and continue cooking for 4 minutes, stirring occasionally, until softened. Add the chicken pieces and cook until evenly browned, turning once or twice, about 8 minutes.

In a medium bowl, combine the curry powder, cumin, coriander, salt, pepper, yogurt and lemon juice and stir well. Scrape the mixture into the frying pan and turn the chicken and onion to combine well.

Reduce the heat to low, cover the pan and simmer, turning the chicken once or twice, until it is tender and cooked through, 50 to 60 minutes.

Stir in the raisins and cashews, transfer to a serving dish, and sprinkle with green onions. Serve hot or warm.

NOTES

⊛ Because it is made with chicken on the bone, which releases natural gelatin, the sauce will thicken to a jelly once it is chilled. Reheat gently and it will melt to its original texture.

⊛ My favorite way to make this curry is to use only legs and thighs, as I prefer dark meat.

⊛ If you prefer to use boneless, skinless chicken, cut it into large pieces and add it to the curry about 20 minutes after you have added the spices and covered the pan. Cover and continue cooking as directed, until the ingredients are well combined and the chicken is cooked through.

THAI GRILLED CHICKEN *with* SWEET *and* SPICY GARLIC SAUCE

Serves 4 to 6

THIS SPECTACULAR DISH IS STANDARD FARE in northeastern Thailand, where street vendors serve it with a pungent dipping sauce, spicy-hot green papaya salad and Sticky Rice (page 166). That makes for an all-finger food meal, perfect for summer picnics or tailgate feasts if you substitute Curry Dip with Crudités (page 23) for the green papaya salad. The chicken needs only an hour or so to marinate, though it can be left in the marinade longer if need be.

3-4 pounds chicken thighs or
      breasts, skin removed
2 tablespoons coarsely chopped
      garlic (8-10 cloves)
2 tablespoons chopped fresh
      cilantro
2 tablespoons soy sauce

1 tablespoon curry powder,
      store-bought or homemade
      (page 222, 224 or 226)
1 teaspoon vegetable oil
1 teaspoon salt
1 teaspoon freshly ground pepper
Sweet and Spicy Garlic Sauce
      (page 232)

Rinse the chicken, pat dry and set aside. In a food processor or in a blender, combine the garlic, cilantro, soy sauce, curry powder, oil, salt and pepper. Pulse to combine well and puree until fairly smooth. Transfer the sauce to a large bowl, add the chicken and toss to coat well. Cover and refrigerate 1 to 24 hours.

Preheat the grill or broiler until very hot.

Place the chicken pieces on the grill or under the broiler and cook for 30 to 35 minutes, turning occasionally, until well browned and cooked through. When the chicken is done, transfer to a serving platter and serve hot, warm or at room temperature with Sweet and Spicy Garlic Sauce.

TANDOORI CHICKEN HOMESTYLE

Serves 4 to 6

UNLESS YOU HAVE A TANDOOR, the enormous, barrel-shaped oven that blasts ferocious heat into the kitchens of many Indian restaurants, you will be unable to duplicate the terrific look and taste of their chicken. You can, however, make a delectable version to be roasted in your oven or cooked on the grill. Paprika and turmeric give this dish a handsome terra-cotta color.

2 teaspoons ground coriander	2 tablespoons coarsely chopped garlic
1½ teaspoons ground cumin	
1 cup plain yogurt	2 teaspoons paprika
¼ cup freshly squeezed lemon juice (about 2 lemons)	1 teaspoon ground turmeric
	1 teaspoon salt
¾ cup coarsely chopped onion	¼ teaspoon freshly ground pepper
2 tablespoons coarsely chopped fresh ginger	3-4 pounds chicken pieces *(see Notes)*

In a small, dry frying pan over medium heat, toast the coriander and cumin for about 2 minutes, until they darken a little and release their aroma, stirring often to prevent them from burning. Tip out onto a plate; cool briefly.

In a blender or food processor, combine the yogurt, lemon juice, onion, ginger, garlic, paprika, turmeric, salt and pepper. Add the toasted coriander and cumin and grind every-thing to a smooth, evenly colored puree, pulsing on and off and scraping down the sides occasionally to mix everything well. Set aside while you prepare the chicken.

Rinse the chicken and pat dry with paper towels. Remove the skin and use a sharp knife to cut 2 or 3 diagonal slashes into each piece of chicken, spacing the slashes an inch or so apart and cutting about 1 inch deep into the breast meat and almost to the bone on legs and thighs.

In a deep bowl or a large, sturdy resealable plastic bag, combine the chicken with the tandoori marinade and toss to mix well. Thoroughly coat each piece, rubbing the marinade into the slits. Cover the bowl or seal the bag tightly and refrigerate for 12 to 24 hours, turning occasionally to marinate the meat well.

When you are almost ready to cook the chicken, preheat the oven to 500 degrees F, and line a roasting pan or a baking sheet with sides with aluminum foil.

Place the chicken pieces on the pan and roast for 15 minutes. Reduce the heat to 400 degrees and roast for another 20 minutes, or until cooked through. Remove from the oven, transfer to a platter and serve at once.

NOTES

⊛ Tandoori chicken can be on the dry side, so you will get the best results by cooking the chicken on the bone. Dark meat is ideal, so you may want to purchase only legs and thighs.

⊛ If you cannot wait 24 hours for this recipe, marinate it as long as you can. Even 3 to 4 hours will give you a good dish, although the longer you leave it, the more tender and flavorful it will be.

⊛ If you prefer to use boneless chicken breasts, pound them lightly and shorten the marinating time to about 2 hours. Roast in the oven or grill for 4 to 5 minutes per side, or until cooked through. Check often to avoid overcooking.

BUTTER CHICKEN

Serves 4

NDIAN CHEFS CREATED THIS RECIPE to make good use of leftover tandoori chicken, which is often on hand at closing time. Tandoori chicken reheats poorly since it is marinated in yogurt and cooked at high temperatures, both of which dry it out.

In this recipe, it is enveloped in a luxurious tomato-cream sauce enlivened with sweet spices. Called *murgh makhani* on Indian restaurant menus, Butter Chicken is rich, but a worthwhile indulgence. I serve it with a crisp green salad and lots of basmati rice.

2½ pounds cooked tandoori chicken (page 98)	½ teaspoon ground cinnamon
4 tablespoons butter, chilled	½ teaspoon ground cardamom
1 tablespoon paprika	¼ teaspoon freshly ground pepper
¼ teaspoon ground turmeric	¼ teaspoon ground cloves
½ teaspoon salt	1 can (14½-ounce) peeled and diced tomatoes, including juice
½ teaspoon ground cumin	½ cup cream

Bone the chicken and tear the meat into bite-size pieces. You will have about 4 cups. Cut the butter into small pieces and set aside in the refrigerator. In a small bowl, combine the paprika, turmeric, salt, cumin, cinnamon, cardamom, pepper and cloves; set aside.

In a large frying pan, bring the tomatoes and their juice to a gentle boil. Add the spices, reduce the heat to maintain a simmer and cook over medium heat, stirring occasionally, until slightly thickened, about 5 minutes.

Add the chicken and cream and stir well. Cook 3 minutes, stirring often, until the sauce is well combined and the chicken is heated through.

Stir in the butter and quickly remove from the heat, stirring gently until the butter is melted and the sauce is smooth. Serve at once.

NOTES

⊛ To keep the sauce from separating, do not let it come to a boil once the butter is added.

⊛ To prepare this dish ahead, cook as directed but omit the final step of stirring in the butter. Cool, cover and refrigerate for several hours. Then reheat gently and continue as directed, stirring in the butter and serving at once.

⊛ You can substitute 2 teaspoons garam masala (page 228 or 230 or store-bought) for the ground cumin, cinnamon, cardamom, pepper and cloves.

⊛ You can make this dish with leftover grilled or roasted chicken as well. Increase the aromatic spices as follows to compensate for the missing tandoori flavors: 1 teaspoon ground cumin, 1 teaspoon ground cinnamon, 1 teaspoon ground cardamom, ½ teaspoon freshly ground pepper and ½ teaspoon ground cloves.

STIR-FRIED CHICKEN *with* TOMATOES *and* GREEN PEPPERS

Serves 4

CURRY POWDER TRANSFORMS THIS SIMPLE STIR-FRY into a satisfying supper. Since it has green peppers and tomatoes, I like to serve it as a one-dish meal over lots of rice. You can also use an equal amount of Indian-style curry paste instead of curry powder.

2 tablespoons vegetable oil	¾ pound boneless, skinless chicken breast
1½ cups thinly sliced onion	
1 cup thinly sliced green bell pepper	3 plum tomatoes, coarsely chopped, or 1 can (15-ounce) ready-cut tomatoes, including juice
1 tablespoon finely chopped garlic	
1 teaspoon peeled, minced fresh ginger	½ teaspoon salt
2 tablespoons curry powder, store-bought or homemade *(page 222, 224 or 226)*	3 tablespoons finely chopped fresh cilantro

In a large frying pan over medium-high heat, heat the oil until a bit of garlic sizzles as soon as you drop it into the pan. Add the onion and cook, stirring often, until it is softened, shiny and beginning to brown, 2 to 3 minutes.

Add the green pepper, garlic, ginger and curry powder and cook, tossing occasionally, until the pepper softens and the mixture is fragrant, about 3 minutes.

Add the chicken and cook 3 minutes, tossing occasionally to mix well and coat the chicken with the curry. Stir in the tomatoes and salt and, if using fresh tomatoes, cover (for canned, cook uncovered). Cook 5 minutes, tossing occasionally, until the tomatoes are softened and the chicken is cooked through.

Remove from the heat, add the cilantro and toss well. Transfer to a serving dish and serve hot or warm.

NOTE

⊕ I also love this dish made with boned chicken thighs, with the skin left on to make a rich sauce. Cook it a little longer if you use dark meat.

OASIS CURRIED CHICKEN

Serves 6

LAMIA ZAHR, CHEF/OWNER OF OASIS MART in Royal Oak, Michigan, kindly shared her recipe for a quick sauté of curry powder and chicken. Served over rice, this curry provides a bright, lemony main course in minutes. See Mail-Order Sources (page 258) for her address to order spices, curry pastes, pickles and condiments for your kitchen pantry.

3 boneless, skinless chicken breasts	1 teaspoon salt
2 tablespoons olive oil	1 cup water
2 large onions, sliced	2 tablespoons freshly squeezed lemon juice
1 garlic clove, chopped	2 tablespoons finely chopped fresh cilantro or parsley
1 tablespoon curry powder, store-bought or homemade *(page 222, 224 or 226)*	

Cut the chicken into bite-size pieces about ¼ inch thick. In a large, heavy frying pan, heat the oil over medium-high heat for about 30 seconds. Add the chicken and cook, stirring often, until lightly browned, about 2 minutes. Add the onions and garlic and cook 2 minutes, stirring occasionally, until the onion is shiny and softened. Add the curry powder and salt and cook 2 minutes, stirring occasionally.

Add the water and simmer until the chicken is cooked, 10 to 15 minutes. Remove from the heat and add the lemon juice and cilantro or parsley. Stir well and let stand 2 to 3 minutes. Serve hot or warm.

Thai Mussamun Curry *with* Chicken, Potatoes *and* Peanuts

Serves 8 to 10

THIS CLASSIC THAI DISH is often served on special occasions. Thai people invite friends and relatives to their homes for a feast in celebration of weddings, births, housewarmings or the ordination of a family member as a Buddhist monk. In this curry, the flavors of cinnamon, cloves, cardamom and nutmeg sing out over the standard Thai chorus of cumin, coriander, peppercorns and dried red chilies. Along with these sweet spices, the inclusion of potatoes, peanuts and tamarind suggests a direct culinary link with the kitchens of India.

This curry comes from southern Thailand, where many Thais follow the teachings of Islam. *Mussamun* is thought to be a pronunciation of the word "Muslim." In Thailand, mussamun curries are often made with chunks of beef, but chicken is popular as well. Make this one a day ahead and you will be rewarded with an extraordinary blossoming of spice-laden flavors. Serve with rice or noodles.

2 cans (each 14-ounce)
   unsweetened coconut milk
   (about 3½ cups), *divided*

3 tablespoons mussamun curry
   paste, store-bought or
   homemade *(page 220)*

2 pounds boneless chicken thighs
   or breasts, cut into bite-size
   chunks, skin left on

1 large potato, peeled and cut
   into bite-size chunks
   (about 1½ cups)

1 medium onion, halved
   lengthwise and sliced
   lengthwise into thick wedges

½ cup dry-roasted salted peanuts

6 cinnamon sticks, each about
   3 inches long

3 tablespoons fish sauce

3 tablespoons palm sugar
   (page 253) or light or
   dark brown sugar

3 tablespoons tamarind liquid
   (page 238); *see Notes*

¼ teaspoon salt

2 tablespoons freshly squeezed
   lime juice, plus more
   if needed

Open 1 can of coconut milk and use a fork to stir the contents until smooth and well combined. In a 6-quart saucepan or Dutch oven, bring ½ cup of the stirred coconut milk to a boil over medium-high heat. Add the curry paste and cook 1 minute, stirring and mashing the paste into the coconut milk. Add the chicken and cook 2 minutes, stirring often, until the chicken begins to change color. Add the potato, onion, peanuts and cinnamon sticks and toss with the chicken. Add all the remaining coconut milk, fish sauce, sugar, tamarind liquid and salt and bring to a boil.

Reduce the heat to maintain a simmer and cook 15 to 20 minutes, until the potato is tender and the chicken is cooked through. Add 2 tablespoons of the lime juice and stir well. Taste and add more, if desired. Remove from the heat and let stand 10 minutes. Transfer to a serving bowl, removing and discarding the cinnamon sticks, or leaving them in as a traditional garnish not to be eaten. Serve hot or warm.

NOTES

❀ Tamarind liquid adds a rich, deep sweet-sour note, but if you do not have this ingredient, the curry will still taste good. Add a little extra lime juice and taste to see that you have a pleasing balance of salty, sour and sweet flavors. Then you can add a bit more salt, lime juice or sugar, if needed.

❀ Traditionally, this curry includes whole toasted cardamom pods. If you have access to them, here is how to include them: Toast a dozen whole pods in a small, dry frying pan over medium heat for several minutes until fragrant and lightly browned, shaking the pan often to avoid burning. Add these to the curry along with the peanuts and cinnamon sticks. Like the cinnamon sticks, the cardamom pods are left in for their flavor and beauty, but they are not eaten. If you are toasting the cardamom, toast the peanuts as well for 3 to 4 minutes, until they are fragrant and lightly browned.

❀ If you are preparing this curry in advance, you may want to postpone adding the potato until the last 5 minutes of cooking time, so that it will remain firm. Cool the curry to room temperature, then cover and chill until shortly before serving time. Reheat gently until the potato is tender and the curry is heated through.

THAI GREEN CURRY *with* SNOW PEAS *and* SHRIMP

Serves 4

THIS IS A BEAUTIFUL CURRY, with pink shrimp and bright green snow peas in a heavenly herb-infused sauce. Try it with bay scallops or small, tender clams when you can find them in the market. If you combine several types of seafood, you can christen the dish Thai Green Curry *Boh Taek*. The Thai words translate as "broken net," denoting a glorious hodgepodge of fresh seafood, bursting from the nets onto the deck of the fishing boat. Serve this warm with rice or noodles.

¼ pound snow peas *(see Notes)*

1 can (14-ounce) unsweetened coconut milk, *divided*

3 tablespoons green curry paste, store-bought or homemade *(page 214)*

1 medium onion, halved lengthwise and thinly sliced crosswise

1 pound medium shrimp, peeled and deveined

12-15 wild lime leaves, if available *(see Notes)*

1 tablespoon palm sugar *(page 253)* or light or dark brown sugar

1 tablespoon fish sauce

Handful of fresh basil

2 tablespoons coarsely chopped fresh cilantro

Trim the snow peas, removing the stem ends.

Open the can of coconut milk and stir it with a fork until smooth and well combined. In a large saucepan, bring ⅓ cup of the coconut milk to a gentle boil over medium-high heat. Add the curry paste and cook 1 minute, stirring and mashing to soften the paste. Add the onion and continue cooking for 2 minutes, stirring often. Reduce the heat to medium and add the shrimp and lime leaves, if using. Cook about 1 minute, stirring often, until the shrimp become pink.

Add the remaining coconut milk, sugar and fish sauce and bring to a gentle boil.

Add the snow peas, stir well and simmer 2 minutes while you cut the basil leaves crosswise into strips. Stir in the basil and cilantro and remove from the heat. Serve warm.

NOTES

⊕ If the snow peas are large, cut them in half lengthwise on the diagonal before adding them to the curry.

⊕ Wild lime leaves, also called kaffir or kefir lime leaves, are an aromatic herbal addition to many curries in Southeast Asian cuisines. If you can find them at an Asian market, toss a handful into any curry. If you cannot find them, do not despair. There is no substitute, but your curry will be delicious without them. (See page 256 for more about wild lime leaves and page 257 for a mail-order source.)

⊕ Try this recipe with about ¾ pound boneless, skinless chicken meat cut into bite-size chunks and 1½ cups eggplant chunks. Cook the chicken as directed for the shrimp, but after the fish sauce is added, simmer for 10 minutes, add the eggplant and simmer for 5 minutes more, or just until the chicken is cooked through and the eggplant is softened. You can omit the snow peas or add them as directed.

CHOO CHEE SHRIMP

Serves 4

TRY THIS QUICK, SIMPLE CURRY when you want an exotic taste of Thailand without a lot of time and trouble. *Choo chee* curry pastes are red curry pastes made without the usual addition of spices—typically cumin, coriander and peppercorns. But any Thai-style curry paste will work fine in this recipe. Try the dish with scallops or with chunks of fish fillet. Serve with plenty of rice.

1 cup canned unsweetened coconut milk, *divided*

1 tablespoon red curry paste, store-bought or homemade *(page 218)*

½ cup water

1 tablespoon fish sauce

1 tablespoon palm sugar *(page 253)* or light or dark brown sugar

Handful of fresh basil

Salt (optional)

¾ pound medium shrimp, peeled, deveined and halved lengthwise

Stir the coconut milk well and divide it into two ½-cup portions. Place 1 portion in a medium frying pan and warm it over medium heat until it comes to a gentle boil. Cook 3 minutes, stirring occasionally, until it thickens a little and releases its fragrance.

Add the curry paste and cook 2 minutes, mashing and stirring to dissolve it and mix it into the coconut milk. Stir in the remaining coconut milk, water, fish sauce and sugar and bring to a gentle boil. Gently boil for 8 to 10 minutes, stirring occasionally, until the sauce is smooth and slightly thickened.

Meanwhile, separate the basil leaves from their stalks, reserving a few sprigs for garnish. Tear very large leaves into 2 or 3 pieces. Taste the sauce and adjust the seasonings to your liking with fish sauce, sugar or a little salt.

Stir in the shrimp and basil leaves and cook until the shrimp curl, turn pink and are cooked through, about 2 minutes. Remove from the heat and transfer to a serving dish. Garnish with fresh basil sprigs, and serve hot or warm.

◀◀◀ ▶▶▶

NOTE

✺ Use Thai basil (page 255) if you can find it, though Italian basil works too. If you have access to fresh wild lime leaves, add them whole with the basil leaves, or slice them crosswise into very thin strips and sprinkle them over the top before serving.

RED CURRY SHRIMP FRIED RICE

Serves 4 to 6

WITH ITS COLORFUL CONFETTI of red, green, yellow and pink, this hearty rice can be the main event or an elegant addition to a buffet. The dish is only moderately hot, so add a tablespoon or more of Thai-style curry paste if you like more fire in your food. Leftover rice works best here, since the grains are firm and separate, so plan ahead. If you have hot rice, spread it out on a baking sheet and chill it in the freezer for about a half hour.

¼ pound snow peas	1 pound medium shrimp, peeled and deveined
½ red bell pepper	
3 cups cold cooked rice (from about 1½ cups raw)	2 tablespoons fish sauce (*see Notes*)
4 tablespoons vegetable oil, *divided*	1 tablespoon soy sauce
2 large eggs, lightly beaten	2 teaspoons sugar
1 cup coarsely chopped red onion	½ cup minced green onions
2 serrano chili peppers, thinly sliced crosswise	½ cup finely chopped fresh cilantro
1 tablespoon red curry paste, store-bought or homemade (*page 218*)	

Trim the snow peas, removing the stem ends and cut them in half lengthwise on the diagonal. Cut the red pepper into long, thin strips. Put the rice into a large bowl and use your fingers to gently break up any clumps and separate into loose grains. Place next to the stove, along with the remaining ingredients and a plate large enough to hold the cooked vegetables and eggs.

Heat a wok or large, deep frying pan over medium-high heat for 30 seconds and add 1 tablespoon of the oil. Swirl to coat the pan and add the snow peas and red pepper. Stir-fry for 30 seconds and remove the vegetables to the plate.

Add 1 tablespoon of oil to the wok and swirl to heat it. Add the eggs, scramble them and transfer them to the plate with the vegetables.

Add the remaining 2 tablespoons oil to the wok and swirl to heat it. Add the onion, chilies and curry paste. Stir-fry until the onion softens and the curry paste is well mixed in, tossing and mashing as the mixture cooks, about 3 minutes. Add the shrimp and stir-fry, tossing often, until they turn pink and become firm, about 1½ minutes. Add the rice, fish sauce, soy sauce and sugar and toss well.

Add the reserved cooked vegetables and eggs and the green onions. Toss well and continue cooking, tossing occasionally, until everything is well combined and the rice is heated through, 3 to 4 minutes. Transfer to a serving platter. Sprinkle with the cilantro and serve hot or warm.

NOTES

⊛ You can substitute 1½ cups frozen peas for the snow peas, adding them frozen, along with the eggs and green onions, at the end of the cooking time. You can also use small broccoli florets, stir-frying them along with the red pepper.

⊛ If you do not have fish sauce, you can substitute 1 additional tablespoon of soy sauce, for a total of 2 tablespoons.

SINGAPORE CURRY NOODLES *with* GREEN PEPPERS *and* SHRIMP

Serves 4 to 6

THIS DELICATE NOODLE STIR-FRY is a standard on the menu at Chinese restaurants that feature dim sum, an array of dumplings and other savory bite-size fare served at lunchtime. While choosing small plates from the carts that are wheeled about the dining room, many diners order a noodle dish or two to round out their brunch Chinese-style.

My friend Joyce Jue, author of many fine cookbooks on Asian cuisines, reports that Singapore noodles are almost unheard of in that country, but got their name because the curry powder in them reminds Asian cooks of the fusion of Chinese, Indian and Malay cooking in the Singaporean kitchen. The thin rice noodles used in this dish are also called rice sticks, or rice vermicelli, and they are widely available in the Asian-ingredients section in supermarkets around the country or by mail (pages 258 and 259). See Notes for a delicious vegetarian version.

1 package (6-ounce) very thin dried rice noodles	1 tablespoon minced garlic
1 green bell pepper	1 cup finely chopped onion
3 tablespoons vegetable oil, *divided*	About ¾ cup chicken broth
½ pound medium shrimp, peeled and deveined	1-2 tablespoons curry powder, store-bought or homemade *(page 222, 224 or 226)*
	1 teaspoon salt

Place the noodles in a large bowl and add warm water to cover by at least 1 inch. Leave them to soften for about 15 minutes.

Meanwhile, cut the green pepper in half lengthwise, pull out and discard the stem and seeds, and cut the pepper into slender strips about 2 inches long. Cut the rounded end sections into thin pieces as well. You will have about 1½ cups. Prepare and measure out all the remaining ingredients and place them by the stove, along with a large serving platter to hold the finished dish.

When the noodles have softened, drain them well and place them on a cutting board. You will have about 4 cups noodles, now weighing about 16 ounces. Mound the noodles into a big log and cut through the log crosswise in 5 places to shorten the noodles, so they will be easier to stir-fry and coat with the ingredients. Using your fingers, gather the noodles into a pile and toss to separate into strands. Set aside near the stove.

Place a wok over high heat for about 15 seconds, then add 2 tablespoons of the oil. Heat for about 30 seconds, until a bit of garlic sizzles wildly as soon as it is dropped into the wok. Add the shrimp and cook, tossing often, until they firm up and turn pink, 1 to 2 minutes. With a slotted spoon, transfer the shrimp to the serving platter, draining them over the wok to leave behind as much oil as possible.

Add the garlic and toss for about 30 seconds, until fragrant but not browned. Add the green pepper and onion and cook, tossing often, until the vegetables are shiny, softened and fragrant, about 2 minutes. Transfer to the serving platter, along with the shrimp.

Add the remaining 1 tablespoon oil to the wok, swirl to coat the wok evenly and add the rice noodles. Toss well and add the broth, pouring it in a circle around the sides of the wok. Cook about 2 minutes more, tossing the noodles often to expose them to the hot broth and heat them through.

Reduce the heat to medium and return the shrimp and onion mixture to the wok, including any juices. Add the curry powder and salt and toss well. Cook the noodles about 2 minutes more, tossing occasionally to combine the ingredients.

When the noodles are tender and evenly coated with the curry powder and have absorbed the broth, transfer them to the platter, pull a few shrimp and green peppers to the top, and serve hot or warm.

NOTES

⊛ Fine rice noodles are widely available in supermarkets in the Asian-food section. Often labeled "rice vermicelli," they look more like fishing line than food, and they are quite brittle and difficult to break. Packages often carry the words *mai fun*, which is the Mandarin Chinese name for them. They look quite similar to *sai fun*, a thin noodle made from mung beans. To be certain you have the ones you want, check the ingredient list to see they are made of rice.

⊛ If you have a larger package of noodles and want to use just part of it, pull the noodles apart inside a paper bag. This keeps you from having to clean up all the tiny pieces that will break off as you pull the skeins apart. Or simply soften the entire package in warm water, measure out the 4 cups you need for this recipe, wrap and refrigerate the unused portion, and use it within 2 days.

⊛ A wok gives the best results when stir-frying a batch of noodles, but a large, deep frying pan will work.

⊛ For vegetarian Singapore Curry Noodles, follow the directions for stir-frying shrimp but use about 3 cups (6 ounces) sliced mushrooms, adding an extra tablespoon oil and cooking the mushrooms for about 3 minutes, until tender, darkened and shiny. Add 2 small zucchini, quartered lengthwise and cut crosswise into triangles, along with the green pepper, and use vegetable broth instead of chicken broth.

Malay-Style Rice Noodles
with Shrimp
in Coconut Curry Soup

Serves 5 to 6

THIS IS MY VERSION of *laksa*, a hearty noodle meal in a bowl enjoyed throughout Southeast Asia. It's a rich yellow curry with shrimp, bean sprouts and fresh herbs in coconut milk.

Fresh spaghetti-size rice noodles, known as laksa, are the traditional choice, but you can use any kind of noodle. Try dried rice noodles or Chinese-style wheat noodles if you have an Asian market handy, or use linguine, spaghetti or fettuccine instead, cooked al dente.

Soup noodle dishes like this one are traditionally served in large, deep soup bowls, with chopsticks for eating the shrimp and noodles and a large Chinese-style soup spoon for savoring the curry. These are available in Asian markets and by mail (see pages 258 and 259). You could serve this dish in deep Italian-style pasta plates, or use small Western-style soup bowls with spoons and forks, dividing everything into smaller batches and offering second helpings to your guests.

1 pound dried rice noodles or rice vermicelli or 1 pound fresh linguine or ¾ pound dried linguine or spaghetti

2 tablespoons yellow curry paste or red curry paste, store-bought or homemade *(page 216 or 218)*; *see Notes*

1 tablespoon finely ground macadamia nuts, cashews, peanuts or pine nuts

1 teaspoon ground turmeric

2 teaspoons water

2 cans (each 14-ounce) unsweetened coconut milk, *divided*

1 can (14-ounce) chicken or vegetable broth (about 1¾ cups)

1 tablespoon palm sugar *(page 253)* or light or dark brown sugar

1 teaspoon salt

1 pound medium shrimp, peeled and deveined

1 bunch fresh mint or basil

1½ cups fresh bean sprouts

3 green onions, thinly sliced crosswise

1 hothouse cucumber, peeled, seeded and cut into 2-inch strips

1 lime, cut crosswise into 6 wedges

Chili garlic sauce or any hot chili sauce *(see Notes)*

If using rice noodles, bring a medium saucepan of water to a rolling boil over high heat. Add the rice noodles and cook until tender but still firm, about 2 minutes, stirring often to separate the noodles and help them cook evenly. Drain, rinse well in cold water, drain again and set aside. If using linguine or other Italian-style pasta, bring a large pot of water to a boil, add the noodles, and cook for 2 to 4 minutes for fresh, 10 to 13 minutes for dried; drain and set aside.

In a small bowl, combine the curry paste, ground nuts, turmeric and water and mash with a fork. In a large, deep skillet, heat ¾ cup of the coconut milk over medium heat until it comes to a gentle boil, stirring often. Cook for about 3 minutes, until the milk thickens a little and bubbles gently. Reduce the heat to low, add the curry-paste mixture and cook, stirring and mashing often, until fragrant, softened and somewhat thickened, about 4 minutes.

Add the remaining coconut milk, broth, sugar and salt, stir well, increase the heat to medium and bring to a gentle boil. Simmer 10 minutes, stirring occasionally.

Add the shrimp. Cook 2 to 3 minutes, stirring occasionally, until the shrimp turn pink and are cooked through. Remove from the heat and set aside.

When you are ready to serve, coarsely chop the mint or basil. Divide the rice noodles and bean sprouts among 5 or 6 large Asian-style soup bowls and add the shrimp curry almost to cover the noodles, using about 1 cup noodles and ¾ cup curry for each serving. Arrange a few shrimp on top of each bowl and garnish with the green onions, cucumber and fresh mint or basil and lime. Serve at once, along with small saucers of chili sauce. Have diners squeeze lime onto their noodles and add chili sauce, if they wish.

NOTES

⊛ If you use red curry paste, you can add 1 teaspoon ground turmeric for a golden color.

⊛ You can use about 1½ cups cooked chicken or another meat, shredded, instead of shrimp. For vegetarian laksa, use vegetable broth, omit the shrimp and instead, briefly simmer 1 cup sautéed salted mushrooms and 1 cup thinly sliced, pressed tofu in the curry sauce until heated through.

⊛ Chili garlic sauce is a fire-engine-red prepared condiment found in many supermarkets and most Asian markets. See page 243 for more information.

⊛ Like all coconut-milk-based stews, this one may separate as it stands. Simply stir well and reheat gently.

GRILLED SWORDFISH STEAKS *in* CILANTRO-GINGER PESTO

Serves 4

THIS FLAVORFUL MARINADE comes together so quickly that you will be amazed at what terrific results you can get from a few minutes of work. It wins raves from guests, and you will probably find yourself making it on a weeknight as well.

⅓ cup olive oil

3 tablespoons freshly squeezed lime or lemon juice

2 tablespoons soy sauce

1 tablespoon honey

1 tablespoon finely chopped garlic

1 tablespoon finely chopped fresh ginger

½ cup chopped fresh cilantro

1 tablespoon curry powder, store-bought or homemade *(page 222, 224 or 226)*

1 teaspoon salt

¼ teaspoon freshly ground pepper

2 pounds swordfish steaks, about 1 inch thick

In a blender or food processor, combine the oil, lime or lemon juice, soy sauce, honey, garlic, ginger, cilantro, curry powder, salt and pepper. Grind until fairly smooth and pour into a baking dish just large enough to hold the swordfish steaks in one layer. Add the swordfish and turn to coat well with the marinade.

Cover and refrigerate for at least 30 minutes and up to 2 hours, turning once if marinating for more than 30 minutes.

Prepare a grill or broiler.

Remove the fish from the marinade and cook 6 inches from the heat source for 7 minutes on one side. Turn and brush with the remaining marinade. Cook the second side for 5 to 7 minutes, until nicely browned and cooked through. Serve immediately

NOTE

❁ To prepare in advance, make the marinade in the morning, cover and refrigerate until close to cooking time. Then combine with the fish and marinate and cook as directed.

CURRIED SCALLOPS
in PARCHMENT PACKAGES

Serves 4

YELLOW CURRY PASTE gives a lovely golden hue to this elegant yet feisty dish, but any Thai-style curry paste, homemade or purchased, will work well. You can cook shrimp, bay scallops or a combination of seafood in the same way, as well as large chunks of firm-fleshed fish, such as red snapper, halibut, sea bass or even catfish. Stir the coconut milk well after opening the can and before measuring out what you need, as it often separates as it sits.

Parchment packets make a beautiful presentation for company and are simple enough to do for a family meal. The packets can be prepared earlier in the day and then kept in the refrigerator until shortly before serving time. Bake them for just 10 minutes in a hot oven while everyone waits at the table for their surprise packages.

You will find parchment paper at cookware stores and well-stocked supermarkets.

¼ cup unsweetened coconut milk	½ teaspoon salt
2 tablespoons freshly squeezed lime juice	1 pound large sea scallops
1 tablespoon Thai-style yellow curry paste, store-bought or homemade *(page 216)*	1 bag (10-ounce) fresh spinach (about 4 cups), washed and stemmed
1 teaspoon sugar	2 green onions, thinly sliced crosswise

In a medium bowl, combine the coconut milk, lime juice, curry paste, sugar and salt and stir well. Add the scallops, toss gently to coat with the marinade, cover and refrigerate for at least 15 minutes and up to 1 hour.

Preheat the oven to 450 degrees F.

To make the parchment packets, cut the parchment paper into 4 rectangles, each 15 inches x 10 inches. Starting at 1 of the short edges, fold each sheet in half and crease it well. Place the folded sheets on a large, clean work surface. Open the crease and place about 1 cup of the spinach leaves in the middle of 1 side of each sheet, dividing the spinach among all 4 sheets. Place a portion of the scallops and their marinade on each nest of spinach, dividing them evenly among the 4 sheets. Sprinkle each portion with the green onions.

To close the packets, fold the top side over the scallops and spinach. Starting at 1 edge, fold the parchment and roll it in, crimping the edge, working along in a curved line until you reach the other side and the entire edge is sealed. This will transform each rectangular sheet of paper into a half-moon. Repeat with the 3 remaining packets.

Arrange the packets carefully on an ungreased baking sheet with sides and place in the oven for 10 minutes. Remove, transfer the packets to individual dinner plates and serve at once, letting each person break into his or her own packet.

NOTE

⊛ Parchment paper is sturdy enough to withstand the heat of the oven without burning. It keeps food flavorful as it cooks. You can substitute aluminum foil if parchment paper is difficult to find.

STEAMED CLAMS
or MUSSELS GOA-STYLE

Serves 4

THIS TASTY SEAFOOD STEAM FEAST from the Indian coastal town of Goa calls for tiny clams, such as Manila clams, which are often available at Asian markets, or cockle clams, which you may find in seafood specialty shops. If you like mussels, use them instead of clams. For an authentic version, add a handful of grated fresh coconut along with the cilantro just before serving, and toss well. Serve with rice or crusty bread so that you can savor the sauce.

2 tablespoons vegetable oil	1 teaspoon salt
2 tablespoons finely chopped garlic	3 pounds Manila or cockle clams or black mussels
2 tablespoons peeled, finely chopped fresh ginger	2 tablespoons water
1 cup finely chopped onion	1 tablespoon freshly squeezed lemon juice
1 tablespoon curry powder, store-bought or homemade *(page 222, 224 or 226)*	½ cup coarsely chopped fresh cilantro

In a large, deep saucepan with a tight-fitting lid, heat the oil over medium heat until a bit of garlic sizzles as soon as it is dropped into the pan. Add the garlic and ginger and toss for 1 minute. Add the onion and cook for 4 minutes, tossing often, until it is shiny, softened and just beginning to brown.

Add the curry powder and salt and toss for 1 minute. Add the clams or mussels and the water. Stir to mix well. Cover tightly, reduce the heat to low and cook 8 to 10 minutes, until most of the shells are open.

Remove from the heat. Add the lemon juice and cilantro and toss well, discarding any shells that have not opened.

Transfer the clams or mussels and their sauce to a serving dish and serve hot or warm.

NOTE

❁ Traditionally, this dish is crowned with a confetti of freshly grated coconut. If you are comfortable opening and grating a fresh coconut, do so. Sprinkle about ½ cup finely grated coconut meat over the steamed clams, along with the chopped cilantro and toss well. Reserve 2 tablespoons of the clear liquid inside the coconut, using it instead of water when adding the clams to the pan.

BURMESE-STYLE PORK CURRY
with FRESH GINGER

Serves 6

THIS EXTRAORDINARY DISH will delight curry fans and convert those who do not yet share your passion. It is a variation on the Northern Thai classic called *gaeng hahng ley*, which long ago crossed the Burmese border to enter Thailand's culinary repertoire, and it exemplifies the Southeast Asian love of sweet, sour and hot flavors in harmony. The absence of coconut milk makes this curry lighter than many other Thai versions, but the sauce is wonderfully rich—and superb on a plate of jasmine rice.

¼ cup peeled, slivered fresh ginger

1½ pounds boneless country-style pork spareribs

2 tablespoons red curry paste, store-bought or homemade *(page 218)*

¼ cup light or dark brown sugar

2½ cups water

2 teaspoons ground turmeric

1 teaspoon dark soy sauce or 2 teaspoons regular soy sauce

½ teaspoon salt

¼ cup thinly sliced shallots

2 tablespoons minced garlic

¼ cup freshly squeezed lime juice

Place the slivered ginger in a small bowl, add warm water to cover and set aside. Cut the pork into 1-inch chunks.

Combine the pork, curry paste and brown sugar in a heavy 6-quart saucepan or Dutch oven. Stir to combine the curry paste and sugar, and coat the pork with the mixture. Place the pan over medium heat and cook for 15 minutes, stirring occasionally, until the pork browns slightly and renders some of its fat.

In a large measuring cup, stir together the water, turmeric, soy sauce and salt, and pour over the pork. Bring to a rolling boil and lower the heat to maintain a simmer. Cook, uncovered, until the meat is tender and the sauce has cooked down somewhat and thickened, 45 to 50 minutes.

Add the ginger with its soaking liquid, along with the shallots, garlic and lime juice. Continue cooking for 5 more minutes. Taste the sauce: it should have a pleasing balance of flavors—salty, sour and sweet. Adjust by adding more salt, lime juice or sugar, if needed. Serve hot or warm.

◀◀◀▶▶▶

NOTE

❁ This curry reheats well. To prepare in advance, cool to room temperature, cover and refrigerate for 1 day. Reheat gently, check the flavors again, adjust as needed, and serve hot or warm.

PORK VINDALOO GOA-STYLE

Serves 6

THIS SHARP, SPICY CURRY comes from the Portuguese communities of Goa, a port city near the southwestern tip of the Indian subcontinent. The dish marries aromatic spices with peppers' heat and vinegar's tang. Increase the amounts of the crushed red pepper and ground peppercorns if you like fiery food. Marinate it for as long as you can—up to 24 hours—and prepare the vindaloo in advance if possible, as its flavor is enhanced with a day's rest and it reheats well. Serve with rice.

1 tablespoon ground cumin	2 tablespoons coarsely chopped garlic
1½ teaspoons crushed red pepper	2 tablespoons coarsely chopped fresh ginger
1 teaspoon ground coriander	½ cup white vinegar or cider vinegar
1 teaspoon ground cinnamon	
1 teaspoon freshly ground pepper	2 pounds boneless country-style pork spareribs
½ teaspoon ground cloves	
½ teaspoon ground cardamom	2 tablespoons vegetable oil or ghee, store-bought or homemade *(page 234)*
1 tablespoon light or dark brown sugar	
2 teaspoons salt	
1 teaspoon paprika	2 teaspoons black or brown mustard seeds *(page 241)*
1 teaspoon ground turmeric	
1 cup coarsely chopped onion	½ cup water

Combine the cumin, red pepper, coriander, cinnamon, pepper, cloves and cardamom in a small, dry frying pan. Place over medium-high heat and toast the spices, stirring often to prevent burning, until they are fragrant and a shade darker, 1 to 2 minutes.

Transfer to a mini food processor or blender. Add the brown sugar, salt, paprika, turmeric, onion, garlic and ginger. If you are using a food processor, puree to a coarse paste, add the vinegar and continue processing to a fairly smooth paste. If you are using a blender, add the vinegar to the onion-spice mixture first and then puree all the ingredients until you have a fairly smooth paste. Stop the processor or blender several times to scrape down the sides as you puree the mixture, 2 to 3 minutes, until fairly smooth. Scrape the vindaloo paste into a large, deep bowl and set aside.

Cut the pork into 1-inch chunks and pat dry. Combine with the vindaloo paste in the bowl and stir to coat the meat well with the paste. Cover and refrigerate 1 to 2 hours.

To cook the curry, remove the meat from the marinade to a plate, using a slotted spoon; reserve the marinade. Pour the oil or ghee into a large, deep saucepan or Dutch oven with a tight-fitting lid. Heat briefly over medium-high heat *(see Note)*, add the mustard seeds and cover at once. Let the seeds pop for 10 to 20 seconds.

Uncover and add the pork. Cook for about 3 minutes, stirring often. Add the reserved marinade and water and stir well. Let the curry come to a rolling boil. Lower the heat to medium and simmer gently until the pork is tender and the sauce is thickened and smooth, 45 to 50 minutes. Serve hot or warm.

NOTE

⊛ When adding the mustard seeds to the oil, the oil should be very warm but not hot, lest the seeds burn and pop out of the pan.

PORK CHOPS *with* CURRIED CHUTNEY SAUCE

Serves 4

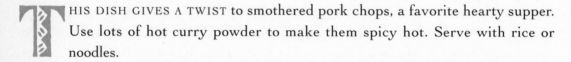

THIS DISH GIVES A TWIST to smothered pork chops, a favorite hearty supper. Use lots of hot curry powder to make them spicy hot. Serve with rice or noodles.

About ¼ cup flour
1 teaspoon salt
¼ teaspoon freshly ground pepper
4 blade-cut pork chops, about 1 inch thick
2 tablespoons butter or vegetable oil
2 tablespoons finely chopped shallots
2 teaspoons curry powder, store-bought or homemade *(page 222, 224 or 226)*

¼ cup Madeira wine, Marsala, cream sherry or white wine
¾ cup chicken broth
¾ cup half-and-half
1 teaspoon cornstarch
½ cup homemade fruit chutney *(see Notes)* or store-bought mango chutney
¼ cup minced chives or green onions

In a shallow dish, combine the flour, salt and pepper and mix well with a fork. Rinse the pork chops, pat dry with paper towels and place them on a plate. Slash the fat edge in several places with a knife to prevent them from curling during cooking. Dredge each chop in the flour mixture, gently shake off the excess flour and set aside on the plate next to the stove, with the remaining ingredients.

In a large, heavy frying pan with a tight-fitting lid, heat the butter or oil over medium-high heat and add the pork chops. Cook until lightly browned, about 1 minute per side. Remove and set aside.

Add the shallots and curry powder to the pan and cook for 2 to 3 minutes, until the shallots are shiny, softened and evenly coated with curry powder. Add the spirits and broth. Bring to a boil, scraping up any browned bits from the bottom of the pan.

In a small bowl, combine the half-and-half and cornstarch and stir well. Add to the frying pan, along with the chutney, and bring to a gentle boil. Reduce the heat to maintain a simmer and cook about 3 minutes, stirring occasionally, until the sauce is golden and slightly thickened.

Return the pork chops to the frying pan, turning them until they are well coated with the sauce. Cover and simmer about 20 minutes, turning after 10 minutes, until the chops are cooked through.

Serve the chops hot or warm, smothered with sauce, and sprinkled with chives or green onions.

NOTES

✸ If you use store-bought mango chutney, cut any large chunks of fruit into small pieces before adding to the pan. Or use Fresh Mango Chutney (page 196), Ginger Pear Chutney (page 191), Apple Raisin Chutney (page 194) or Fresh Fig Chutney (page 190).

✸ You can prepare this dish several hours in advance, reserving the chives or green onions until serving time. Complete the recipe, cool briefly, and cover and refrigerate until shortly before serving time. Then reheat gently until the chops are heated through and the sauce is bubbly and hot. Garnish and serve as directed.

THAI RED CURRY *with* BEEF, EGGPLANT *and* RED BELL PEPPER

Serves 4

THIS DISH IS SO SPEEDY that you will be amazed at how wonderful it tastes. Consider it a blueprint for an array of other curries, substituting chicken or pork for the beef, and other quick-cooking vegetables, such as green beans, carrots, mushrooms or zucchini, for the eggplant and red bell pepper. If you keep the basics on hand, you can prepare a Thai curry in the time it takes a pot of rice to cook. Stock up on Thai curry paste, canned or frozen coconut milk and fish sauce and you will be ready for spontaneous, Thai-inspired curry feasts. If you do not have fish sauce, add a dash of soy sauce and a teaspoon of salt instead. Serve with rice or noodles.

1 can (14-ounce) unsweetened coconut milk, *divided*

2 tablespoons red curry paste, store-bought or homemade *(page 218)*, *divided*

1 pound beef top sirloin, sliced crosswise into thin, bite-size strips

1 tablespoon vegetable oil

1 cup chopped onion

1 small eggplant, peeled and cut into ¾-inch cubes (about 4 cups)

3 tablespoons fish sauce

½ cup fresh basil

1 red bell pepper, cut into bite-size pieces

Open the can of coconut milk and use a fork to stir the contents until smooth and well combined. Place a plate by the stove. In a medium saucepan over medium-high heat, bring about ¼ cup of the coconut milk to a boil. Add 1 tablespoon of the curry paste and stir-fry for about 30 seconds, stirring and mashing to soften the paste and combine it with the coconut milk.

Add the beef and cook 1 to 2 minutes, just until it changes color. Remove it to the plate with a slotted spoon, leaving as much curry as possible behind in the saucepan.

Add the oil and remaining 1 tablespoon curry paste to the pan and cook about 30 seconds, stirring and mashing as you did before. Add the onion and eggplant and cook 2 to 3 minutes, stirring often, until the onion is softened and shiny. Add the remaining coconut milk and the fish sauce and bring to a boil. Lower the heat to maintain a simmer and cook, uncovered, 7 to 8 minutes, or until the eggplant is tender.

Meanwhile, slice the basil crosswise into shreds and set aside. When the eggplant is tender, return the beef to the saucepan and add the red pepper. Simmer until the beef is heated through, about 2 minutes. Stir in the basil and remove from the heat. Serve hot or warm.

PANAENG BEEF CURRY *with* PEANUTS *and* FRESH BASIL

Serves 4

PANAENG CURRIES are on my shortlist of favorite Thai curries. Cooks differ on the exact components of a panaeng curry paste but agree that it is a red one, made with dried red chilies as the fiery foundation. What makes panaeng curries sublime is not the paste itself, but the unusual cooking method. They are made with less coconut milk than usual so they are quite thick, and they are enriched with the addition of a handful of finely chopped peanuts at the end. Any Thai-style curry paste will work well in this recipe. If you can find fresh wild lime leaves, slice them crosswise into very thin strips and scatter them over the top of the curry before serving.

3 tablespoons vegetable oil

2 tablespoons panaeng or red curry paste, store-bought or homemade *(page 218)*

¾ pound thinly sliced beef *(see Note)*

1 can (14-ounce) unsweetened coconut milk, *divided*

2 tablespoons fish sauce

1 tablespoon palm sugar *(page 253)* or light or dark brown sugar

¼ teaspoon salt

¼ cup dry-roasted salted peanuts, finely chopped

½ red bell pepper, sliced into long, thin strips

Fresh basil sprigs

In a large frying pan over medium heat, combine the oil and curry paste. Cook 3 to 4 minutes, adjusting the heat to keep the paste sizzling gently without popping and splashing, and mashing and scraping the paste to soften and warm it. Add the beef and cook 2 to 3 minutes, separating the pieces to coat them with the paste and brown them evenly.

Stir the coconut milk well and add 1 cup to the frying pan. Bring to a gentle boil over medium heat and cook for about 10 minutes, adjusting the heat to keep it simmering gently.

Add the remaining coconut milk, fish sauce, sugar, salt and peanuts. Cook gently about 5 more minutes, stirring occasionally. Add the red pepper strips and stir them into the curry. Taste and adjust the seasonings, adding salt or sugar as needed.

Transfer to a small, shallow bowl and garnish with the basil. Serve hot or warm.

◀◀◀ ▶▶▶

NOTE

⊛ I like to use flank steak or beef sirloin, sliced crosswise into thin strips about 2 inches long.

LAMB CURRY KASHMIRI-STYLE

Serves 4 to 6

THIS IS MY VERSION of *rogan josh*, an earthy lamb curry, aromatic with fennel seed and cardamom. Its robust, deep-red gravy calls for mountains of basmati rice or a stack of chapatis (page 176) warm from the stove. The cooking is uncomplicated, and once you have measured out all the spices, you will soon be rewarded with a tasty curry. Make this dish a day in advance. You can substitute 2 pounds lean boneless lamb cut into large, bite-size chunks for the chops.

1 tablespoon paprika
1 teaspoon ground fennel
1 teaspoon ground ginger
1 teaspoon salt
½ teaspoon ground cumin
½ teaspoon ground coriander
½ teaspoon ground cardamom
¼ teaspoon ground cinnamon
¼ teaspoon ground turmeric
Pinch ground cayenne pepper
3 tablespoons vegetable oil or ghee, store-bought or homemade *(page 234)*
12 whole cloves
5 cardamom pods

3 cinnamon sticks, each about 3 inches long
2 tablespoons finely chopped garlic
1 tablespoon peeled, finely chopped fresh ginger
2 cups coarsely chopped onion, *divided*
3 pounds lamb shoulder chops, bone-in
¾ cup plain yogurt
2½ cups water
1 small bunch fresh cilantro, finely chopped

In a small bowl, combine the paprika, fennel, ginger, salt, cumin, coriander, cardamom, cinnamon, turmeric and cayenne pepper. Stir to mix well and set aside by the stove.

Heat the oil or ghee in a large, deep saucepan for 1 minute over medium heat. Add the cloves, cardamom pods and cinnamon sticks and cook 1 minute. Add the garlic and ginger and cook until fragrant and shiny, tossing often, about 1 minute. Add 1 cup of the onion and cook, tossing often, 3 to 4 minutes, until it is shiny, softened and fragrant.

Place a platter by the stove and increase the heat to medium-high. Add the lamb chops in batches and brown each batch for 5 minutes, turning once. Transfer each batch to the platter.

When you have browned all the lamb, reduce the heat to medium and add the spice mixture. Stir well for about 30 seconds to toast the spices and then add the yogurt. Stir well to combine it with the spices and bring to a gentle boil. Return the lamb to the pan and toss to coat with the yogurt and spices. Add the water and the remaining 1 cup onion and let the curry come to a rolling boil. Stir well, reduce the heat to maintain an active simmer and cook 45 to 50 minutes, until the lamb is tender and the sauce is thickened.

Remove the meat and set it out on a platter to cool. Remove and discard the bones and fat, and chop the meat into large, bite-size chunks. Return the meat to the curry sauce and stir well. Remove the whole spices, if you like, or keep them in as a traditional garnish not to be eaten. Serve hot or warm, sprinkled with the cilantro.

◀◀◀▶▶▶

NOTE

⊛ If you are preparing this dish in advance, cover and chill it overnight. Before reheating, skim off and discard the fat that will have congealed on the surface of the curry. Reheat gently and serve hot.

CHAPTER 5

VEGETABLES AND SIDE DISHES

THESE RECIPES INVITE YOU to bring vegetables to the center of the plate. The chapter begins with my version of the simple and delicious lentil porridge called dal. Ubiquitous throughout India in both palaces and humble homes, dals are made from the array of lentils and dried beans available in Indian markets. Also called pulses, these little protein powerhouses are a cornerstone of Indian vegetarian cooking.

Vegetarianism in India reaches back thousands of years to the foundations of Hinduism. Within this culinary tradition, you will find inspired uses of herbs and spices in an imaginative variety of savory dishes. Green Pea Curry with

Fresh Paneer Cheese is a classic vegetarian dish, known in Hindi as *mattar paneer*. Enjoy it with a bowl of dal and either a stack of warm chapatis or a rice pilaf studded with cinnamon sticks, cardamom pods and whole cloves.

The strong vegetarian traditions found in India are not echoed in Thailand. But adapting Thai cuisine to accommodate vegetarian cooks is a simple matter, as in New Potatoes and Red Bell Peppers in Fresh Green Curry.

OTHER DISHES in this chapter move outside the realm of traditional cooking in various ways. Curried Black-Eyed Peas with

Eggplant is hearty Indian-inspired fare for a chilly day. Vegetable Ravioli with Toasted Walnuts in Curry Cream Sauce, a California-style dish with a burst of curry powder, is lovely for company yet simple to cook. Roots and Wings brings heaven and earth together with a fanciful spin on sweet potatoes and curly kale. Like most of the dishes in this chapter, it can be a main course, a side dish or one of several dishes on a curry-inspired buffet.

Vegetables *and* Side Dishes

CREAMED CORN *with* CILANTRO *and* GREEN PEPPERS

Serves 6 to 8

WHEN SWEET CORN fills the summer produce stands, make this with about four cups of kernels cut right off the cob. Chop up a fresh green serrano chili and add it with the green pepper if you like things hot.

2 tablespoons butter	¼ teaspoon freshly ground pepper
¾ cup chopped onion	1 bag (16-ounce) frozen corn
¾ cup chopped green bell pepper	kernels (4 cups), thawed
1 tablespoon curry powder,	3 tablespoons half-and-half
store-bought or homemade	2 tablespoons finely chopped
(page 222, 224 or 226)	fresh cilantro
½ teaspoon salt	

Melt the butter in a medium frying pan over medium-high heat. When the butter is bubbly, add the onion, green pepper, curry powder, salt and pepper and cook 2 minutes, tossing occasionally, until the vegetables are shiny, fragrant and evenly coated with the curry powder.

Add the corn and half-and-half, cover and cook 2 minutes, tossing occasionally to combine well.

Remove from the heat, add the cilantro and toss well. Serve hot or warm.

NEW POTATOES *and* RED BELL PEPPERS *in* FRESH GREEN CURRY

Serves 4 to 6

HERE IS A QUICK VEGETARIAN CURRY, bright with fresh herbs. This curry paste takes only a few minutes, but you can make it even simpler by using any store-bought paste, Thai- or Indian-style, instead of grinding your own.

1 pound new potatoes, unpeeled, about 2 inches in diameter	3 tablespoons plus 1 cup water, *divided*
1 red bell pepper	¾ cup coarsely chopped fresh cilantro leaves and stems, *divided*
2 tablespoons coarsely chopped shallots	
1 tablespoon coarsely chopped garlic	1 can (14-ounce) unsweetened coconut milk, *divided*
1 teaspoon peeled, coarsely chopped fresh ginger	1 teaspoon palm sugar *(page 253)* or light or dark brown sugar
2 fresh jalapeño chili peppers or 1 fresh serrano chili pepper	1 teaspoon salt
	¼ cup fresh basil

Halve the potatoes. Halve the red pepper lengthwise, discard the stem and seeds, and cut into 1-inch chunks. Set aside.

In a small food processor or blender, combine the shallots, garlic, ginger, chilies and 3 tablespoons water. Add ½ cup of the cilantro. Grind until you have a fairly smooth paste, pulsing and stopping often to stir down the sides and incorporate all the ingredients.

You will have about ¼ cup curry paste; set aside.

Open the coconut milk and stir well until smooth. Pour ½ cup coconut milk into a medium saucepan and place over medium heat. When it comes to a boil, reduce the heat to low and gently boil 3 minutes, stirring occasionally, until slightly thickened.

Add the curry paste and cook, stirring and mashing, until it is dissolved into the coconut milk and heated through, about 2 minutes. Add the remaining coconut milk, remaining 1 cup water, sugar, salt and potatoes. Increase the heat to high and bring the curry to a rolling boil. Stir well, reduce the heat to maintain a gentle boil and continue cooking, uncovered, for 10 to 15 minutes, until the potatoes are tender and the sauce is smooth and a soothing green throughout.

Meanwhile, chop the basil leaves crosswise into thin strips, reserving a sprig or two for garnish. When the curry is cooked, stir in the basil, the red peppers and the remaining ¼ cup cilantro. Remove from the heat and serve hot or warm, garnished with basil sprigs.

NOTES

⊛ You will need a total of about 1½ cups canned or frozen coconut milk. If you make fresh coconut milk from scratch, omit the 1 cup of water that is added to the canned coconut milk, and use a total of 2½ cups of your own freshly made coconut milk.

⊛ To substitute prepared curry paste, omit the shallots, garlic, ginger, chili pepper, cilantro and the 3 tablespoons water, and begin by cooking 2 tablespoons prepared curry paste in coconut milk.

⊛ If you can find only big new potatoes in the market, use them, cutting them into walnut-size chunks.

VEGETABLE RAVIOLI *with* TOASTED WALNUTS *in* CURRY CREAM SAUCE

Serves 4 to 6

MAKE THIS PASTA FOR YOUR NEXT GATHERING, either as the main course or as a hearty vegetarian addition to a buffet. Try the sauce with other pasta shapes, including any noncheese-stuffed pasta such as tortelli or tortellini, or with the plump potato dumpling pillows called gnocchi, which are often available frozen in Italian markets.

½ cup coarsely chopped walnuts

1½ teaspoons salt, *divided*

2 packages (each 9-ounce) fresh vegetable ravioli

2 teaspoons vegetable oil

¼ cup unsalted butter

3 tablespoons minced shallots

2 teaspoons curry powder, store-bought or homemade *(page 222, 224 or 226)*

1 cup vegetable broth

1 cup whipping cream or cashew milk *(page 233)* or unsweetened coconut milk

¼ cup minced fresh chives or thinly sliced green onions

Preheat the oven to 350 degrees F.

Place the walnuts in a cake pan or pie tin. When the oven is hot, toast the walnuts 6 to 8 minutes, stirring often, until fragrant and lightly browned. Transfer to a plate to cool.

Bring a large, covered pot full of water to a rolling boil over high heat. Add 1 teaspoon of the salt. When the water returns to a rolling boil, add the ravioli. Cook 4 to 5 minutes, until just tender but still firm, as they will cook another minute or two in the curry sauce. Drain the ravioli well, transfer to a large, shallow serving bowl, toss with the oil and set aside.

In a large frying pan over medium-high heat, melt the butter, turning to coat the pan and prevent burning. When the butter is foamy, add the shallots and curry powder and cook until the shallots are tender, about 2 minutes. Add the broth and boil for about 10 minutes, stirring occasionally, until you have about ½ cup.

Add the cream or milk and the remaining ½ teaspoon salt and bring to a rolling boil. Cook until slightly thickened, stirring occasionally, about 3 minutes. Add the ravioli to the sauce and cook 1 to 2 minutes to heat through, stirring occasionally.

Return the ravioli to the serving bowl, along with the sauce, sprinkle with the toasted walnuts and the chives or green onions, and serve hot or warm.

DAL

Serves 2 to 4

DALS ARE LENTIL DISHES seasoned with garlic, onion and spices and cooked into a rich puree. This version cooks quickly, improves if it is made ahead and re-heated and complements any curry or grilled dish. Enjoy its luscious sauce with rice or any griddle bread.

Masoor dal is the salmon-pink lentil, widely available in health-food stores as well as in Indian markets. It is one of the quickest-cooking varieties of lentils. You could substitute other types, allowing a little extra time for them to cook.

½ cup raw red lentils (masoor dal)

3 cups water

1 teaspoon salt

½ teaspoon ground turmeric

¼ teaspoon ground cayenne pepper

2 tablespoons vegetable oil or butter

½ teaspoon cumin seeds

½ teaspoon asafetida *(page 240)*; *see Notes*

1 tablespoon finely chopped garlic

1 tablespoon peeled, finely chopped fresh ginger

½ cup finely chopped onion

½ cup finely chopped tomato

Rinse and drain the lentils and combine with the water in a medium saucepan. Stir in the salt, turmeric and cayenne and bring to a rolling boil over medium heat. Skim off and discard the cloudy white foam that appears on the surface as the lentils begin to boil. Reduce the heat to low and simmer, uncovered, for 20 minutes, stirring occasionally to prevent sticking.

Meanwhile, heat the oil or butter in a medium frying pan over high heat for about 30 seconds. Add the cumin seeds and the asafetida and cook for 1 minute, until the seeds begin to sizzle and pop. Add the garlic, ginger, onion and tomato and toss gently for 1 minute, until they shine and begin to wilt. Reduce the heat to medium and cook 5 minutes, tossing occasionally. Set aside.

Add the onion mixture to the lentils and continue cooking 5 to 10 minutes, or until the lentils are cooked. Stir well and remove from the heat. Serve hot or warm.

NOTES

⊛ This dal is thick and a little chunky, thinner than mashed potatoes but thicker than oatmeal. It thickens as it stands, so thin with a little water if you are reheating it.

⊛ Many traditional recipes call for whisking the cooked lentils to mash them and create a smoother texture. Try this if you like, either before or after you add the cooked onion.

⊛ You can omit the asafetida.

ROOTS *and* WINGS

Serves 6 to 8

THIS SPICY COMBINATION of sweet potatoes and kale is the creation of Kelley Worrell, a San Diego-based chef with a passion for natural foods. Sweet potatoes are the roots, and she began seeing humble kale as wings the year her garden produced a bounty of tender, green leaves, which seemed to sprout from the ground aiming to take flight.

This combination of earthbound curried sweet potatoes and winged kale in a light, sweet-sour dressing looks great, tastes even better than it looks, keeps beautifully for several days and is delicious warm, at room temperature or cold. For vegetarians, it can be a centerpiece dish as well as a side dish. More chili flakes will help you crank up the heat on this spicy number.

Sweet Potatoes and Kale

4-6 sweet potatoes (about 3 pounds)
¼ cup soy sauce
2 tablespoons olive oil
2 tablespoons minced garlic
2 tablespoons curry powder, store-bought or homemade (*page 222, 224 or 226*)
1 teaspoon salt
½ teaspoon freshly ground pepper
½ teaspoon crushed red pepper
1 bunch kale
2 cups water

Dressing

2 tablespoons rice vinegar
2 tablespoons honey
¼ teaspoon crushed red pepper

Make the Sweet Potatoes and Kale. Preheat the oven to 400 degrees F.

Peel the sweet potatoes and slice them crosswise into ½-inch-thick rounds. Place them in a large bowl and toss with the soy sauce, oil, garlic, curry powder, salt, pepper and red pepper. Place on a parchment- or foil-lined baking sheet and bake, turning once, until they are tender when pierced with a fork and beginning to brown, about 45 minutes. Remove them from the oven and let cool about 20 minutes.

Meanwhile, wash the kale, slice it into ½-inch strips and place it in a large bowl. Bring the water to a rolling boil and pour it over the kale. Toss with tongs or 2 forks until the leaves are wilted and bright green. Drain the kale well and place in large, dry bowl.

Make the Dressing. In a small bowl, whisk together the vinegar, honey and red pepper.

Add the dressing to the kale and toss. When the sweet potatoes have cooled, combine them with the kale and toss to coat everything well with the dressing. Serve warm or at room temperature.

NOTE

◉ Sweet potatoes about 2 inches in diameter are ideal for this recipe.

GREEN PEA CURRY
with FRESH PANEER CHEESE

Serves 4 to 6

THIS IS MY VERSION of the Indian vegetarian classic, *mattar paneer*. Tomatoes, onions, fresh Indian-style cheese and a handful of herbs and spices transform green peas from cafeteria fare into an exciting, lightly sauced vegetarian dish.

Vegetable oil for frying

2 cups paneer cheese cubes
   (page 236)

3 tablespoons vegetable oil
   or ghee, store-bought or
   homemade *(page 234)*

1 cup finely chopped onion

1 tablespoon peeled, minced
   fresh ginger

1 tablespoon minced garlic

2 teaspoons ground coriander

1 teaspoon ground cumin

1 teaspoon salt

½ teaspoon ground turmeric

¼ teaspoon ground cayenne
   pepper

1 cup canned diced tomatoes,
   including juice

½ cup water

1½ cups frozen green peas

½ cup finely chopped fresh
   cilantro

Pour the oil into a medium frying pan to a depth of about 2 inches. Place a slotted metal spoon and a plate lined with paper towels next to the stove. Heat the oil over medium-high heat until very hot, about 360 degrees F. When a bit of paneer cheese sizzles as soon as you drop it into the pan, the oil is ready. Carefully add about one-third of the chunks of paneer, and gently stir to turn and separate them as they cook. As soon as the cheese is evenly browned, 30 seconds to 1 minute, remove with the slotted spoon, hold over the pan to drain, and place on the paper-towel-lined plate. Continue cooking the remaining cheese and set aside to drain and cool.

In a large frying pan over medium-high heat, heat the 3 tablespoons of oil or ghee until a bit of garlic sizzles as soon as you drop it into the pan. Add the onion, ginger and garlic and cook, stirring often, until the onion is shiny, fragrant and beginning to soften, 3 to 5 minutes.

Add the coriander, cumin, salt, turmeric and cayenne and cook 2 more minutes, stirring occasionally to combine the spices with the onion. Add the tomatoes and cook 2 more minutes, stirring occasionally.

Add the fried cheese, water and peas and bring to a boil. Reduce the heat to maintain a simmer and cook 10 minutes more, until the sauce is slightly thickened and smooth. Remove from the heat and stir in the cilantro. Serve hot or warm.

NOTES

⊛ Frying the cheese softens it and helps it absorb the curry flavors from the sauce. But if you prefer not to fry it, you can add it unfried, or sauté it in a small amount of oil until lightly browned.

⊛ If you do not eat dairy foods or lack the time to make up a batch of paneer, you could make a tasty dish substituting pressed tofu for paneer. You can buy pressed tofu in Asian groceries, or press it yourself as directed for paneer on page 237 or use firm tofu and stir gently to discourage it from crumbling.

⊛ I like peas very lightly cooked, so I sometimes stir them in at the end along with the cilantro, rather than cooking them in the sauce. If using fresh peas, add with the tomatoes and check for doneness.

CURRIED GREEN BEANS
with TOMATOES *and* BACON

Serves 4 to 6

ENJOY THIS BRIGHT, QUICK SAUTÉ with any spicy curry or with tandoori chicken and basmati rice.

1 pound fresh green beans	1 tablespoon curry powder, store-bought or homemade *(page 222, 224 or 226)*
1 teaspoon salt, *divided*	
4 slices bacon	1 can (14½-ounce) diced tomatoes, including juice
¾ cup chopped onion	¼ teaspoon freshly ground pepper

Bring a medium saucepan half full of water to a rolling boil over high heat. Meanwhile, trim the green beans. When the water boils, add ½ teaspoon of the salt and the green beans. Cook the beans for 5 minutes, drain, rinse them in cold water to halt their cooking and drain well. Set aside.

Cut the bacon into small pieces and place in a large frying pan. Cook over medium-high heat until crisp, browned and fragrant, about 5 minutes. Drain on paper towels and set aside.

Pour off all but 1 tablespoon of the bacon grease. Add the onion and curry powder and cook over medium heat for about 5 minutes, tossing often, until the onion is tender, shiny and evenly coated with the curry powder. Stir in the tomatoes and cook about 1 minute, until the sauce comes to a gentle boil.

Add the beans and toss well. Continue cooking until the beans are heated through, about 3 minutes. Crumble the bacon and add it to the frying pan along with the remaining ½ teaspoon salt and pepper. Serve hot or warm.

NOTE

❀ You can get a head start on this dish by cooking and cooling the green beans ahead and then covering and refrigerating them overnight.

CURRIED BLACK-EYED PEAS
with EGGPLANT

Serves 6

HERE ARE BLACK-EYED PEAS, a favorite from my Southern childhood, made exotic in terms of flavor yet accessible in terms of ingredients and techniques. Serve this hearty legume dish with basmati rice, Tomato Cucumber Relish (page 201) and a hot Mexican-style tomato salsa for a vegetarian feast.

1 medium eggplant
  (about 1 pound)
1 medium onion
¼ cup vegetable oil
½ teaspoon salt
1 tablespoon finely chopped garlic
2 tablespoons mild Indian-style
  curry paste or 1 tablespoon
  red curry paste, store-bought
  or homemade *(page 218)*

1 teaspoon garam masala, *divided*
  (page 228 or 230); *see Notes*
¼ cup dry red wine
1 can (15-ounce) black-eyed peas,
  rinsed and drained
1 cup canned diced tomatoes,
  including juice
1 cup vegetable broth

Prepare the eggplant by trimming and discarding the ends and quartering it lengthwise. Cut each piece crosswise into ¼-inch slices and set aside. Halve the onion lengthwise, slice lengthwise into thin strips and set aside.

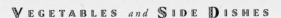
In a large, heavy saucepan or Dutch oven, heat the oil over medium-high heat for 1 minute. Add the eggplant and cook, tossing, for 1 to 2 minutes to coat it evenly with the oil. Sprinkle with the salt and cook 10 minutes, stirring often, until the eggplant is soft. Reduce the heat to medium, add the onion, garlic, curry paste and ½ teaspoon garam masala and stir well. Cook 10 minutes, stirring often, until the onion is shiny, fragrant and tender.

Increase the heat to medium-high, add the wine and simmer, stirring often, until the mixture softens into a thick stew, about 5 minutes. Add the black-eyed peas, tomatoes and broth and bring to a gentle boil. Reduce the heat to low and simmer 15 minutes, stirring occasionally, until the black-eyed peas are heated through and the liquid is reduced.

Remove from the heat, transfer to a serving dish and sprinkle with the remaining ½ teaspoon garam masala. Let it stand a few minutes and serve hot or warm.

NOTES

⊛ If you do not have garam masala, in a small bowl, combine ¼ teaspoon each of ground cloves, ground cinnamon, ground black pepper, ground cardamom and ground cumin in place of the 1 teaspoon garam masala. Stir well and add as directed, half along with the onion and half when the dish has finished cooking.

⊛ Black-eyed peas are widely available canned, frozen and dried. Frozen black-eyed peas can be substituted for the canned. To use dried black-eyed peas, soak them overnight, drain, rinse, cover with fresh water and cook 30 to 40 minutes, or until tender. Use as directed.

New Delhi Garbanzos

Serves 8

CANNED GARBANZOS MAKE THIS HEARTY VEGETARIAN DISH a snap to prepare. While it simmers, you can cook a pot of rice or roll out a batch of chapatis (page 176).

¼ cup vegetable oil

2 medium sweet potatoes, peeled and cut into ½-inch cubes (about 1½ cups)

4 celery stalks, sliced crosswise into ½-inch chunks (about 2 cups)

1 large onion, chopped into ½-inch chunks (2 cups)

2 tablespoons finely chopped garlic

3 tablespoons curry powder, store-bought or homemade *(page 222, 224 or 226)*

2 tablespoons finely chopped fresh basil or 2 teaspoons dried thyme

2 cans (each 15-ounce) diced tomatoes, including juice (about 3 cups)

2 cans (each 20-ounce) garbanzo beans, rinsed and drained (about 4 cups)

1½ cups dried currants or raisins

3 cups vegetable broth

½ cup pine nuts

About ½ teaspoon salt

Heat the oil in a large saucepan over medium heat. Add the sweet potatoes and cook 5 minutes, tossing often, until they are glazed on all sides. Add the celery and onion and cook about 10 minutes, stirring often, until the celery is tender and the onion is transparent.

Add the garlic, curry powder and basil or thyme and stir well. Reduce the heat to medium-low and cook 15 minutes, stirring occasionally. Add the tomatoes, garbanzo beans, currants or raisins and broth and simmer 30 minutes, stirring occasionally.

Meanwhile, toast the pine nuts in a small, dry frying pan over medium heat, tossing often to prevent burning, until lightly browned and fragrant, 3 to 4 minutes. Transfer to a plate and set aside to cool.

When the garbanzo stew is ready, remove from the heat, stir in the salt and taste, adding a little more if needed. Transfer to a serving bowl, sprinkle with the toasted pine nuts, and serve hot or warm.

NOTES

⊛ Garbanzo beans, also called chickpeas, channa and ceci beans, are available both canned and dried. Cooking dried garbanzo beans requires overnight soaking and an hour or more of cooking time. You will need to cook about 1½ cups of dried garbanzo beans to make the 4 cups cooked beans needed in this dish.

⊛ You could also toast the pine nuts in a 375-degree oven for about 5 minutes, stirring occasionally, until fragrant and golden.

CURRIED FRESH FRUIT COMPOTE

Serves 8

THIS OLD FAVORITE from my mother's kitchen is a winner on any holiday buffet table, though it is a shame to wait for a holiday to enjoy its sunny color and sweet-savory taste. It makes a delicious accompaniment to roasted or grilled meats. For an express-lane version, you can substitute canned fruit throughout and still have a winning dish.

3 medium peaches (about 1½ pounds)	¼ cup butter or margarine
2 medium pears (about ¾ pound)	½ cup light or dark brown sugar
2 medium apples (about ½ pound)	1 tablespoon curry powder, store-bought or homemade *(page 222, 224 or 226)*
1 can (4-ounce) pineapple chunks	
10 maraschino cherries	

Preheat the oven to 375 degrees F.

Peel and pit the peaches and cut them lengthwise into thick slices. Transfer to a 13-x-9-inch baking pan. Peel and core the pears and apples, cut them into bite-size chunks and add them to the baking pan. Drain the pineapple chunks, reserving ⅓ cup juice for the curry sauce, and add them to the baking pan, along with the maraschino cherries.

Melt the butter or margarine in a small saucepan over medium heat. Add the brown sugar, curry powder and reserved pineapple juice and cook gently until the sugar is dissolved and the sauce is smooth, about 3 minutes. Pour over the fruit and toss gently to mix well and coat the fruit.

Bake for about 45 minutes, stirring once, until the sauce is bubbly and the fruit is evenly colored and tender. Serve hot or warm.

◀◀◀◀ ▶▶▶▶

NOTE

⊛ To substitute canned fruit, use 1 can (29-ounce) sliced peaches and 1 can (16-ounce) pear halves instead of fresh. Drain the peaches and pears, discarding or reserving the juice for another use, and chop the pears into large chunks. Reduce the baking temperature to 325 degrees and bake for about 30 minutes, stirring once.

CHAPTER 6

RICE AND BREAD

 LEARNED HOW SATISFYING RICE can be during the three years when I lived in rural Thailand working as a Peace Corps volunteer. Rice was the heart of every meal, and I was initially astonished by the amounts consumed by my students and friends. We began each meal by piling everyone's plate with jasmine rice, its delicate, nutty fragrance already filling our kitchen. Most of us enjoyed a second large helping and sometimes even a third. Even at breakfast, a meal little different in content from lunch and dinner in most of Asia, rice was the main attraction in homes rich and poor. Enlivened by bites of omelet, spoonfuls of catfish and lemongrass soup, chunks of cucumber with pungent chili-laced sauces called *nam prik*, and, of course, dollops of fiery curries, rice brought harmony and balance to the roller coaster of flavors that make up Thai food.

I encountered the homey pleasures of my other favorite companions to curries—rustic flatbreads—after moving to Southern California, where the delights of traditional Mexican cooking are always near at hand. Mexican tortillas, whether made from soft wheat flour or nubbly cornmeal, fresh off a comal or reheated on my own stove, are always welcome on the side. I adore the breads of India as well, from griddle-cooked chapatis to the scrumptious pillowy rounds called pooris.

IN THIS CHAPTER, you will find guidance on cooking rice and bread aplenty to fortify your curry-inspired feasts. Start off with plain rice, either Jasmine Rice from Thailand or Basmati Rice, the elegant, needlelike grain harvested at the base of the Himalaya Mountains. Steam up a pot of long-grain Laotian-style Sticky Rice when you want to eat with your fingers, or perfume your kitchen with cinnamon sticks and cardamom pods by making Yellow Rice Pilaf with Whole Spices.

Curried Couscous with Tomatoes and Zucchini brings a Middle Eastern touch to your table in minutes, whenever you need a curry meal in a flash.

You will also find recipes for a quartet of breads, including two classic Indian wheat breads: chapatis and pooris. The pride I feel on turning out a batch of warm flatbreads is exceeded only by the praise I receive from those who materialize in the kitchen to snatch them from the pan.

Rice *and* Bread

Basmati Rice

Serves 3 to 4

THIS AROMATIC RICE grows only in the foothills of the Himalayas and is prized throughout the Indian subcontinent and the Middle East for its delicate texture, aroma and taste. For the best price, buy a 10-pound bag at an Indian or Middle Eastern market. Health-food stores sell basmati rice in bulk, and many well-stocked supermarkets carry this "queen of grains" in 1-pound boxes.

1 cup basmati rice	½ teaspoon salt
2 cups water	

Rinse the rice and drain it well. In a medium saucepan with a tight-fitting lid, bring the water to a rolling boil over high heat. Add the rice and salt, let the water return to a boil, stir well and cover.

Reduce the heat to low and simmer 20 minutes without lifting the lid. Remove from the heat and let stand, covered, 5 minutes.

Uncover and fluff gently with a fork. Serve hot, warm or at room temperature.

NOTES

⊛ For a larger batch, use 2 cups rice, 3 cups water and 1 teaspoon salt. This will make about 4 cups, serving 5 or 6.

⊛ This rice reheats well. Sprinkle with water, cover, leaving a vent for steam to escape, and microwave at high power for 3 to 4 minutes.

INDONESIAN-STYLE RICE PILAF

Serves 3 to 4

THIS IS MY VERSION of *nasi kuning*, the traditional golden rice pilaf served at festivals in Indonesia. It is often shaped into a tall cone symbolic of a mountain sacred to followers of the Hindu religion.

If you don't have lemongrass, leave it out or add 3 wide strips of lime or lemon zest.

1	cup long-grain white rice	1	stalk fresh lemongrass
¾	cup unsweetened coconut milk	3	quarter-size slices fresh ginger
¾	cup water or vegetable or chicken broth	½	teaspoon salt
		½	teaspoon ground turmeric

Wash the rice and drain it well. Combine it with the remaining ingredients in a medium saucepan with a tight-fitting lid. Bring to a rolling boil over high heat.

Stir well, cover, reduce the heat to low and simmer 20 minutes without lifting the lid. Remove from the heat and let stand, covered, for 10 minutes. Uncover and fluff gently with a fork. Remove and discard the lemongrass and ginger. Serve hot or warm.

NOTE

⊛ While the rice is hot, you can mold it into a cone or dome shape by pressing it firmly into a bowl, placing a plate on top of the bowl, and carefully inverting the rice onto it. Garnish with fresh cilantro sprigs or thinly sliced green onions.

Jasmine Rice

Serves 4 to 6

JASMINE RICE GROWS IN THE LUSH PADDY FIELDS of central Thailand and is treasured around the world for its subtle nutty aroma and its delicate texture and taste. This top-quality long-grain rice is increasingly available in supermarkets, health-food stores and specialty-food shops, as well as in Asian markets.

In the Asian tradition, jasmine rice is cooked without seasoning, but you can add butter and salt if you like. Look for texmati, jazmati, wild pecan, popcorn rice and other naturally aromatic strains, which have been bred to thrive in the rice-growing regions of the United States, and are widely available in supermarkets, health-food stores and gourmet specialty shops.

2   cups jasmine rice or other long-grain white rice

3   cups cold water

Rinse the rice well in cold water; drain. Combine the rice and water in a medium saucepan with a tight-fitting lid. Bring to a rolling boil over high heat.

Stir well, reduce the heat to low, cover and simmer for 20 minutes without lifting the lid. Remove the pot from the heat and let it stand, covered, for 10 minutes.

Uncover and fluff gently with a fork. Serve hot, warm or at room temperature.

STICKY RICE

Serves 4 to 6

ALSO KNOWN AS GLUTINOUS, OR SWEET, RICE, sticky rice is eaten morning, noon and night by the people of Laos and the northeastern region of Thailand known as Issahn. Long-grain sticky rice is sold in many Asian markets in the West. It needs soaking before cooking, so plan ahead.

To steam sticky rice in the traditional way, soak it in cold water for at least 3 hours and as long as overnight, then steam it over wildly boiling water for 30 to 45 minutes, until it is sticky, chewy and tender. To enjoy it the traditional way as finger food, begin by serving yourself a fist-size chunk. Pinch off a walnut-size piece and roll it between your fingers into a smooth little lump. Now dip it in sauces, pair it with chunks of meat or vegetable, or eat it "neat."

2 cups long-grain sticky rice

Soak long-grain sticky rice in cold water to cover by at least 2 inches, for 3 hours or more.

Drain the soaked rice and place it in a bamboo steaming basket or other container suitable for steaming. Place a large serving platter next to the steamer on which to cool the cooked rice.

In the base of the steamer, bring 5 to 6 inches of water to a rolling boil. Carefully place the container of sticky rice over the steaming water. Soak a clean kitchen towel (not terry cloth) in water, squeeze it out and fold it to cover the surface of the rice as it steams. Reduce the heat to maintain a steady flow of steam and cook 30 to 45 minutes, until the rice plumps up and changes color from flat, bright white to ivory. Check to see that you can roll and squeeze a spoonful of rice into a small, sticky lump.

Remove from the heat and quickly turn the rice out of the steaming basket and onto the platter. Wet a large spoon or rice paddle and use it to gently spread out the rice into an even layer to cool and dry a little.

As soon as the rice is cool enough to touch, gather it gently into a large ball and transfer to a covered serving basket or onto a serving plate covered with a clean kitchen towel. Keep at room temperature until serving time. Serve hot, warm or at room temperature.

NOTES

❀ Asian markets often carry traditional sticky-rice steamers, which consist of a cone-shaped basket that nestles snugly into a barrel-shaped steaming pot made of lightweight metal. These are inexpensive and do the job beautifully. You can also use a large Chinese-style bamboo steamer tray that fits into a wok. Use a clean kitchen towel (not terry cloth) soaked in water to line the steamer before you add the soaked rice. You can improvise by using a large fine-mesh strainer or a colander that fits into a pot of water while holding the rice suspended above the water during cooking. The pot must enclose the rice container completely so that the steam will be forced through it rather than escaping out the sides.

❀ The cooking time depends on how long you soaked the rice as well as how long ago it was harvested. The longer it soaks and the more recently it was harvested, the quicker it will cook.

❀ Sticky rice does not keep well once it is cooked, so try to enjoy it within a day.

Yellow Rice Pilaf *with* Whole Spices

Serves 4

GOLD IS AN AUSPICIOUS COLOR throughout Southeast Asia, so cooks use turmeric to give rice dishes a golden sheen for special occasions. The whole spices are left in and served along with the dish but not usually eaten. If you have time, slice up an onion or two, fry until crispy golden brown and sprinkle over the pilaf, along with the cilantro leaves.

2 cups basmati, jasmine or other long-grain white rice	1 tablespoon coarsely chopped garlic
3 tablespoons butter or vegetable oil	1 teaspoon peeled, finely chopped fresh ginger
1 cup coarsely chopped onion	1 teaspoon ground turmeric
5 whole cloves	3 cups water
5 green or white cardamom pods	1 teaspoon salt
1 stick cinnamon, about 3 inches long	Handful of fresh cilantro

Rinse the rice in cold water, drain well and set aside. In a medium saucepan with a tight-fitting lid, heat the butter or oil over medium heat and add the onion, cloves, cardamom pods and cinnamon stick. Cook, stirring often, until the onion is shiny and slightly softened, about 1 minute.

Add the garlic, ginger and turmeric. Cook about 2 minutes, stirring often, until the garlic is fragrant but not browned and the onion is evenly colored by the turmeric.

Increase the heat to medium-high and add the rice to the pan. Cook, stirring, for about 2 minutes to color the rice and mix it with the onion. Add the water and salt and stir well. Increase the heat to high, and when the water comes to a rolling boil, stir once more, cover tightly and reduce the heat to low. Cook 20 minutes, without lifting the lid. Remove from the heat and let stand, covered, for 10 minutes.

Uncover, fluff gently with a fork and transfer to a serving platter. Remove the whole spices, if you prefer, or leave them in as a traditional garnish not to be eaten. Sprinkle with the cilantro and serve hot, warm or at room temperature.

RICE *and* RED LENTIL PILAF

Serves 4

THIS IS MY VERSION of *kichiri*, a satisfying traditional dish from India. The dish can be varied to suit your pleasure and make use of what you have on hand. Toss in sliced serrano chilies or ground cayenne for heat, add chopped green onions at the end for color and aroma, vary the spices, omit them or use curry powder instead, or cook the pilaf in broth instead of water. Serve with curry, or pair it with an omelet or a hearty soup for a simple supper.

Red lentils change from their gorgeous sunset color to yellow once they are cooked, and they cook extremely quickly. You can try this recipe with the tiny yellow lentils called *moong dal*, which are the centers of hulled mung beans. You can use other kinds of lentils if you cook them separately, decreasing the amount of water you use in the rice, and then combine the cooked rice and lentils just before serving.

2 tablespoons ghee, store-bought or homemade *(page 234)*, or vegetable oil	¾ teaspoon ground cumin
	½ teaspoon ground turmeric
	¼ teaspoon ground coriander
2 tablespoons chopped garlic	1 cup long-grain white rice
1 tablespoon peeled, chopped fresh ginger	½ cup red lentils
	3 cups water
1 cup chopped onion	½ cup chopped fresh cilantro
1 teaspoon salt	

In a large frying pan with a tight-fitting lid, heat the ghee or oil over medium-high heat until a bit of onion dropped into the pan sizzles at once. Add the garlic and ginger and toss until shiny and fragrant, about 30 seconds. Add the onion and cook, tossing occasionally, until it is shiny, tender and fragrant, about 3 minutes. While the onion is cooking, combine the salt, cumin, turmeric and coriander in a small bowl, stir to mix well, and set aside by the stove.

When the onion is ready, add the spice mixture and cook 1 minute, tossing often to toast the spices and combine them with the onion. Add the rice and lentils and cook 3 minutes, tossing often to mix well.

Add the water and bring to a rolling boil. Stir well, reduce the heat to low and cover the pan. Cook 20 minutes, without lifting the lid. Remove from the heat and let stand, covered, for 10 minutes.

Uncover, fluff gently with a fork, stir in the cilantro and serve hot or warm.

RICE PILAF *with* GOLDEN ONIONS, CASHEWS *and* PEAS

Serves 6 to 8

THIS PILAF DECORATES YOUR TABLE as an appealing accompaniment to any curry or as a main-course grain dish for vegetarian meals. The onions take a little time and care, but the result of your effort is a treat.

3	medium onions	4	cups vegetable broth
½	cup unsalted butter, *divided*	1	teaspoon salt
2	cups long-grain white rice	½	cup frozen peas, thawed
2	cinnamon sticks, each about 3 inches long	¾	cup dry-roasted salted cashews

Cut the onions in half lengthwise. Slice each half crosswise into ½-inch-thick half circles.

In a medium frying pan with a tight-fitting lid, melt ¼ cup of the butter over medium heat, turning the pan to keep it from browning. Add the onion slices and toss to coat well with the butter. Continue cooking, stirring occasionally to separate them into strips until they begin to brown, about 10 minutes. Cover and continue cooking 10 to 15 minutes, until the onions are golden brown and very tender, stirring often to prevent burning. Set aside.

Prepare the rice, using a 2-quart saucepan with a tight-fitting lid. Heat the remaining ¼ cup of butter in the saucepan over medium-high heat until melted and bubbly. Add the rice and cinnamon sticks and sauté, stirring constantly, until most of the rice grains turn white, about 3 minutes. Stir in the broth and salt and bring to a rolling boil. Stir well and cover the pan. Reduce the heat to low and cook 20 to 25 minutes, without lifting the lid, until the rice is tender and the water is absorbed.

Add the peas and cashews and toss well. Turn the rice pilaf out onto a serving platter, remove the cinnamon sticks, mound up the rice and arrange the onions on top. Discard the cinnamon sticks or place them on top as a traditional garnish not to be eaten. Serve hot or warm.

◀◀◀▶▶▶

NOTE

❀ You can prepare the onions several hours ahead, cover and refrigerate. To serve, reheat gently on the stove or in the microwave and arrange on top of the rice.

CURRIED COUSCOUS
with TOMATOES *and* ZUCCHINI

Serves 4 to 6

COUSCOUS, A TINY, GRAINLIKE PASTA, is delicious in its own right, but it is especially valuable to cooks in a hurry. On those days when it is out of the question to roll out fresh chapatis or even wait for rice to cook, couscous is ready in little more than the time it takes a pot of water to boil. Here the couscous is brightened with zucchini, tomatoes and a splash of curry powder. Use it as a light main course or a beautiful and substantial side dish.

2¾ cups water

1 box (10-ounce) quick-cooking couscous (about 1¾ cups dry)

1 teaspoon salt, plus more if needed

1½ cups frozen peas

½ cup pine nuts

3 tablespoons vegetable oil

1½ cups coarsely chopped onion

2 tablespoons coarsely chopped garlic

2 small zucchini

3 plum tomatoes, coarsely chopped

2 tablespoons curry powder, store-bought or homemade *(page 222, 224 or 226)*

½ cup finely chopped fresh cilantro

In a medium saucepan over high heat, bring the water to a rolling boil. Stir in the couscous, salt and peas; cover and remove from the heat. Let stand at least 5 minutes, undisturbed.

Meanwhile toast the pine nuts in a medium, dry frying pan over medium heat 4 to 5 minutes, tossing often to prevent burning, until golden and fragrant. Transfer to a small plate and set aside to cool. In the same pan over medium-high heat, combine the oil, onion and garlic and cook, stirring occasionally, until the onion is shiny and fragrant, about 4 minutes. Meanwhile, trim the zucchini and cut it lengthwise into quarters and then crosswise into ¼-inch slices.

Add the zucchini, tomatoes and curry powder to the frying pan and continue cooking 3 to 4 minutes, stirring occasionally, until the curry coats the vegetables evenly and the zucchini is tender.

Uncover the couscous, fluff it with a fork and transfer to a large bowl. Add the curried vegetables, toasted pine nuts and cilantro and toss well, until the couscous is evenly and brightly colored with the curry. Taste and add salt, if needed. Serve hot, warm or at room temperature.

CHAPATIS

Makes 12 chapatis

CHAPATIS ARE A CLASSIC FLATBREAD OF INDIA, made from a finely ground whole-wheat flour called *atta*. Atta is available in Indian grocery stores or from mail-order sources (pages 257 and 258). My recipe combines the coarser whole-wheat flour available in the West with white flour, which makes a good substitute for the traditional atta.

¾ cup whole-wheat flour	½ teaspoon salt
½ cup white flour	½ cup warm water

In a sifter over a medium bowl, combine the whole-wheat flour, white flour and salt, and sift to combine well.

Add the water and use your hands to mix it into the flour, making a soft dough. Transfer to a lightly floured board and knead for 5 to 7 minutes, turning often and adding flour as needed, until it is smooth, elastic and no longer sticky. Cover with a damp cloth or plastic wrap and set aside to rest for 30 minutes.

To cook the chapatis, roll out the dough into a thin log and cut into 12 pieces. Roll each piece between your palms into a smooth ball. Keep the pieces covered while you roll out the rest one by one. Flatten each ball into a thick disk, place it on a lightly floured surface and roll it out into a thin cake, 4 to 5 inches in diameter.

In a medium frying pan over medium-high heat, cook the chapatis one at a time, turning after about 1 minute and cooking the second side for 30 seconds to 1 minute. Press quickly and firmly at various points around the surface to encourage it to puff. Don't press where it is already bubbling.

Remove and set aside, covering it with a clean kitchen towel to keep it warm. Continue cooking the remaining chapatis, stacking them under the towel, and serve hot or warm.

NOTES

⊛ To substitute atta flour for the combination of whole-wheat and white flour called for in this recipe, use a total of 1¼ cups atta flour and the same amounts of water and salt given here. See page 241 for more information on atta flour.

⊛ To prepare the dough in advance, seal it in an airtight container and keep refrigerated for up to 1 day. About 30 minutes before you plan to use the dough, remove it from the refrigerator and let it come to room temperature.

MELLY'S WHOLE-WHEAT TORTILLAS

Makes 16 to 18 tortillas

Y FRIEND MELLY makes these delicious tortillas. Soft and irresistible when freshly cooked, they reheat beautifully and complement any curry as well as making a terrific breakfast with butter and jam.

1 tablespoon water	⅓ cup vegetable oil
4 tablespoons butter	¾ cup hot water, plus more
3 cups whole-wheat flour	if needed
1 teaspoon salt	White flour for rolling
½ teaspoon baking powder	out tortillas

Combine the water and butter in a small frying pan and heat over medium heat until the butter is melted.

In a large bowl, combine the whole-wheat flour, salt and baking powder and mix well. Add the oil and stir with a wooden spoon until the mixture begins to come together. Using your hands, scoop the flour mixture into a dough, and add the melted-butter mixture and the hot water. Mix, squeeze, knead and mash into a soft dough, using both hands and working the dough vigorously. Add a little more hot water if needed to bring the dough together. When the dough is almost ready, it will pull away from the sides of the bowl and easily form a soft, smooth ball. Twist it, squash it with your fist and turn it over, working it for 3 to 5 minutes, until it springs back when pushed in with your finger, is smooth and has a nice sheen.

Divide the dough into 16 portions and shape into balls. Roll each piece between your palms into a smooth ball, keeping the balls covered with a kitchen towel. Set aside.

Flatten 1 ball into a 3-inch disk and dust with a little white flour. Roll it out into a 7-inch round, turning it clockwise as you roll, flipping it over once or twice.

Heat a large frying pan over medium-high heat until very hot. Test it by adding a drop of water to the pan. If the water sizzles and disappears almost instantly, the pan is ready. Put in 1 tortilla and cook about 30 seconds. Turn it over and continue cooking 1 to 2 minutes, until it begins to bubble and puff up and its color begins to change. Turn the tortilla and press quickly and firmly in several places around the surface to encourage it to puff. Don't press where it is already bubbling. Turn it again to check that it has browned a little and is done.

Remove and set aside, covering it with a clean kitchen towel to keep it warm. Continue cooking the remaining tortillas, stacking them under the towel. Serve hot or warm, or reheat gently in a frying pan on top of the stove.

NOTE

❀ The dough can be refrigerated for up to 1 day, sealed airtight. Let it sit at room temperature to warm up a little before rolling it out.

CURRY CORN BREAD
SOUTHERN-STYLE

Serves 9 to 12; makes 10 to 12 muffins

PAN OF WARM CORN BREAD adds sunshine to your table without a lot of work. Jazz it up with green bell peppers, or try finely chopped jalapeños and more curry powder.

4 tablespoons butter	1 large egg
½ cup finely chopped onion	1 cup yellow cornmeal
½ cup finely chopped green bell pepper	1 cup flour
1 tablespoon curry powder, store-bought or homemade *(page 222, 224 or 226)*	⅓ cup sugar
	1 teaspoon baking powder
	½ teaspoon baking soda
1 cup buttermilk	¾ teaspoon salt

Preheat the oven to 400 degrees F. Grease an 8- or 9-inch-square pan or a muffin tin big enough for 12 muffins, and set aside.

In a medium frying pan over medium heat, melt the butter and add the onion, green pepper and curry powder. Cook for about 3 minutes, tossing occasionally, until the vegetables are shiny, softened and evenly coated with the curry powder. Set aside.

Combine the buttermilk and egg in a small bowl and beat well. In a medium bowl, combine the cornmeal, flour, sugar, baking powder, baking soda and salt and stir to combine well. Add the curried onion mixture and the beaten buttermilk and egg and stir just until the dry ingredients are moistened and the batter is fairly smooth.

Pour the batter into the greased pan and bake for about 20 minutes, until the corn bread is firm and golden brown and a toothpick inserted in the center comes out clean. Cool in the pan 10 minutes. Cut and serve hot, warm or at room temperature.

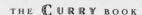

POORIS

Makes 16 small pooris

POORIS ARE A CLASSIC BREAD OF INDIA, made from the same dough as chapatis but deep-fried rather than cooked on a hot griddle. Frying turns the simple wheat dough into delicate, hollow and tasty pillows, which will disappear from your table as fast as you can cook them. The poori pockets are perfect for scooping up luscious curries, grilled foods and sparkling chutneys. Have a slotted metal spoon and a pair of small tongs or two slotted spoons handy when you fry them.

Pooris are at their best when freshly cooked, so it is ideal to have the rest of your meal ready and give them your undivided attention when it is time to cook them.

¾ cup whole-wheat flour	½ cup warm water
½ cup white flour	About 2 cups vegetable oil,
½ teaspoon salt	for frying

In a sifter over a medium bowl, combine the whole-wheat flour, white flour and salt, and sift to combine well.

Add the water and use your hands to mix it into the flour, making a soft dough. Transfer to a lightly floured board and knead for 5 to 7 minutes, turning often and adding flour as needed, until the dough is smooth, elastic and no longer sticky. Cover with a damp cloth or plastic wrap and set aside to rest for 30 minutes.

To cook the pooris, roll out the dough into a thin log and cut into 16 pieces. Roll each piece between your palms into a smooth ball, keeping the balls covered while you roll out the rest. Place a platter or baking sheet by your work space to hold the rolled pooris in a single layer.

Flatten 1 ball into a thick disk, place it on a lightly floured surface and roll it out into a pancake, about 3 inches in diameter. The pancakes should be about ¼ inch thick, like leather, so that they will puff nicely. Place the poori on the platter and continue rolling out the remaining balls.

In a medium frying pan over medium heat, bring the oil to frying temperature, about 360 degrees F. Prepare a platter lined with paper towels on which to place the cooked pooris. Test the oil by dropping a small pinch of dough into the pan. When it sizzles and floats to the surface immediately, the oil is ready.

Gently slide a poori into the oil, and as soon as it begins to puff, use a slotted metal spoon to press it gently into the oil. Move your spoon around the edge, pressing in different spots to help it puff evenly, and turn it over gently as soon as the first side browns, 15 to 30 seconds. As soon as the second side browns, remove the poori from the oil with the slotted spoon or tongs, drain briefly and set it aside on paper towels while you continue cooking the remaining pooris. Serve at once.

NOTES

⊛ You can substitute a total of 1¼ cups atta flour for the whole-wheat and white flour called for here. See page 241 for more information on atta flour.

⊛ To prepare the dough in advance, seal it in an airtight container and keep refrigerated for up to 1 day. Remove about 30 minutes before you plan to use it to let the dough warm to room temperature.

⊛ If you prefer larger pooris, divide the dough into only 8 or 10 balls, taking care not to roll them too thin. Try to make them about as thick as leather or pancakes, rather than paper-thin.

⊛ Pooris are best served very hot and freshly made, but they remain puffed for about half an hour, deflating somewhat as they cool to room temperature. To reheat them, wrap them loosely in foil and place in a 300-degree F oven for 10 to 15 minutes. They will not return to their former glory, but they will still be warm, soft and very good.

CHAPTER 7

CHUTNEYS, RAITAS, RELISHES AND COOLING DRINKS

HERE IS WHERE YOU CAN quench the fires of your curry creations, with a rainbow of condiments that can be made in advance. The classic chutney enjoyed in the West is mango chutney, a child of the British Raj era, which caught the fancy of Anglo-India and has since won converts around the world. This chunky jam is made from green, unripe mangoes sweetened generously with sugar and studded with raisins or currants and familiar curry spices.

The traditional chutneys of India are usually fresh, liberally spiced and often savory and hot. Classics include both raw and cooked versions, made from such ingredients as fresh mint, fresh cilantro, green, unripe mangoes, tomatoes, walnuts and salty dried shrimp. Sweeter chutneys include date, prune, mango and a smoky tamarind chutney laced with toasted cumin.

In this chapter, you will find recipes for a few traditional chutneys and an array of fruity inspirations. They vary in texture, from a pureed Cilantro Mint Chutney to a thin, jamlike Ginger Pear Chutney and a thick Apple Raisin Chutney.

Raitas, vegetables or fruits enrobed in spiced yogurt, also provide a cool contrast to curries. Like salsa, raitas are served in a small bowl, to be scooped up in flatbread or dolloped on rice. I have included recipes for Cucumber Raita, Banana Raita with Toasted Coconut and Fresh Mint and Beet Raita with a fuchsia color that will add a wild beauty to your meal along with its appealing taste. Each of these is simple to stir up at the last minute and will keep for a day or two if covered and chilled.

THE RELISHES IN THIS CHAPTER include my version of the traditional *cachumber*, a chunky mixture of cucumbers, tomatoes and onions in a sprightly lime dressing, which is reminiscent of the fresh tomato salsas of Mexico. You will also find Sweet and Sour Cucumber Salad, a Thai-style pickle not unlike the refrigerator pickles enjoyed in the southern United States all summer long. In Thailand, this *arjaht*, or pickle-salad, is invariably served to accompany satay with peanut sauce, its astringent flavors providing the perfect balance to the sweet luxury of spicy peanut sauce.

Look for Indian-style pickles in Indian markets and mail-order catalogs or in Indian cookbooks. Lime pickle, garlic-date pickle, fresh ginger pickle, carrot-mustard seed pickle and other sharp-flavored condiments offer still other irresistible counterpoints to curry flavors. I have found the quality of store-bought Indian-style pickles and chutneys to be excellent, and I like to keep them handy for brightening and complicating menus with a mere twist of the wrist.

At the end of this chapter, you will find recipes for simple beverages. They provide cool, sweet notes guaranteed to soothe the spiced-out palate. Among the unscientific "cures" we hot-food lovers bandy about as a means of quenching fires, I have heard praise for both dairy products and sugar. Experiment with my version of the yogurt lahssie, a sweet and fruity yogurt smoothie, and an extraordinary sweet green summer beverage made from the slender, spearlike leaves of fresh lemongrass, the queen of Southeast Asian herbs.

Chutneys, Raitas, Relishes *and* Cooling Drinks

BANANA TAMARIND CHUTNEY

Makes about ¾ cup

ADDING CHUNKS OF RIPE BANANA to tamarind chutney makes a tangy accompaniment for grilled meats and for mild or five-alarm curries. Bananas don't keep well, so add them just before serving and enjoy this while it's fresh. I love this cooling chutney paired with Pork Vindaloo Goa-Style (page 128) or with Curried Couscous with Tomatoes and Zucchini (page 174) for a vegetarian meal.

1 firm, ripe banana	1 tablespoon chopped fresh
⅓ cup tamarind chutney	cilantro
(page 192)	

Peel the banana, halve it lengthwise and cut crosswise into ½-inch chunks. Place the banana chunks in a medium bowl with the tamarind chutney and stir to combine well.

Transfer to a small serving bowl and sprinkle with the cilantro. Serve at room temperature. Cover and chill for up to 1 day.

NOTE

❂ Tamarind chutney can separate as it sits, so stir well to restore its thick texture.

CILANTRO MINT CHUTNEY

Makes ¾ cup

THIS SPRIGHTLY FRESH HERB PUREE lights up a plate of steaming grains and softens the flame of the most incendiary curry. Use it as a relish with any curry dish, or as a dipping sauce for flatbreads. Add more serrano chili if you like. Fresh mint chutneys are traditionally quite tart, but the addition of pineapple lends a sweet, fruity note to this tangy South Asian condiment. If you are using canned pineapple, look for pineapple packed in juice rather than heavy syrup.

1 bunch fresh cilantro	1 tablespoon coarsely chopped garlic
1 bunch fresh mint	
1 serrano chili pepper, stemmed and coarsely chopped	1 can (4-ounce) crushed pineapple, including juice, or ½ cup finely chopped fresh pineapple
1½ tablespoons peeled, coarsely chopped fresh ginger	¼ teaspoon salt

Remove and discard the stems of the cilantro and mint, and place their leaves in a food processor or blender. Add the chili pepper, ginger and garlic and grind about 1 minute, stopping once or twice to scrape down the sides, until the herb mixture becomes a fairly smooth puree. Add the pineapple and salt and grind briefly to combine well.

Transfer to a bowl and serve at room temperature. To store, transfer to a jar, seal airtight and refrigerate 4 to 5 days.

FRESH FIG CHUTNEY

Makes about 2¼ cups

WE ENJOY THIS EXTRAORDINARY, smoky-flavored chutney as summer fades into fall, when our backyard fig tree treats us to baskets of sweet green figs. Black Mission figs work beautifully as well. Michele Anna Jordan, a Northern California writer who is author of *The Good Cook's Book*, kindly shared the recipe. She pairs the chutney with grilled duck, roast pork or cream cheese and crackers. I love it with New Delhi Garbanzos (page 156) or as a dip paired with Curried Fresh Corn Fritters (page 28) or Crispy Lamb Wontons (page 32).

1	dozen small (2-inch) fresh figs	1	tablespoon freshly squeezed lemon juice
3	medium garlic cloves		
½	cup dry white wine	1	teaspoon salt
1½	teaspoons ground cumin	½	teaspoon ground cayenne pepper
3	tablespoons cider vinegar		
		¼	cup chopped fresh cilantro

Remove and discard the figs' stem ends and tips. Chop the figs coarsely. Transfer to a blender or a food processor.

Add the garlic and wine, and blend until fairly smooth. Transfer to a medium mixing bowl and set aside. Toast the cumin in a small, dry frying pan over medium heat for about 1 minute, until slightly darker and fragrant. Add to the bowl of fig puree, along with the vinegar, lemon juice, salt, cayenne and cilantro. Stir well, taste and adjust the seasonings to your liking. Serve at room temperature. Cover and chill for up to 3 days.

G INGER P EAR C HUTNEY

Makes 2½ cups

F RESH GINGER gives this chutney a rich depth of flavor that goes beautifully with roast meats. Make up a jar or two for friends you want to please. For a vegetarian feast, set out a small bowl of Ginger Pear Chutney to jazz up Indonesian-Style Rice Pilaf (page 164), Curried Black-Eyed Peas with Eggplant (page 154) and Sweet and Sour Cucumber Salad (page 202).

4	medium, firm pears (about 2 pounds), any kind	1	cup finely chopped onion
½	cup dark raisins	2	tablespoons peeled, minced fresh ginger
¾	cup dark brown sugar	½	teaspoon salt
¾	cup cider vinegar		

Peel, core and dice the pears. Combine them in a heavy medium saucepan with the raisins, brown sugar, vinegar, onion, ginger and salt and stir. Place over medium-high heat and bring to a rolling boil. Stir well, reduce the heat to low and simmer, stirring occasionally, 45 to 50 minutes, until the mixture thickens and softens to the consistency of jam or preserves.

Remove from the heat and let cool to room temperature. Transfer to a jar, seal airtight and refrigerate for up to 2 weeks. Bring to room temperature before serving.

TAMARIND CHUTNEY

Makes about ¾ cup

THE DARK FLAVOR OF TAMARIND lends its sweet-sour punch to this piquant traditional sauce. Serve this in a small bowl along with Chicken Curry (page 94) and Rice Pilaf with Golden Onions, Cashews and Peas (page 172). Guests can spoon Tamarind Chutney over a portion of their rice and mix it in to sharpen the curry flavors. Or offer it with Cilantro Mint Chutney alongside Tandoori Chicken Homestyle (page 98).

⅓ cup tamarind pulp (*see Notes*)	¼ teaspoon ground cayenne pepper
¾ cup warm water	1 tablespoon light or dark brown sugar
½ teaspoon ground cumin	⅛ teaspoon salt

Place the tamarind pulp in a medium mixing bowl and add the warm water. Using your fingers or a large spoon, break the tamarind into lumps, exposing more of its surface to the water. Allow it to soften for about 20 minutes, mashing and stirring it occasionally.

Meanwhile, place the cumin in a small, dry frying pan. Toast it over medium-high heat for about 30 seconds, stirring often and shaking the pan to avoid burning. When the cumin is fragrant and a bit darkened, scoop it out onto a saucer to cool.

Place a large strainer over a medium bowl and pour in the tamarind mixture. Squeeze the tamarind well, working over the lumps to release as much of its fruity essence as possible, separating it from the seeds, pods and fibers in the pulp. Rub the tamarind against the strainer basket well, releasing as much liquid as possible. Scrape the outside of the basket as well to include any puree clinging to it. Discard the remaining mass of seeds, pods and fibers. You will have about ¾ cup of thick, dark puree, about the consistency of applesauce or hot fudge sauce.

Stir in the cumin, cayenne, brown sugar and salt. Serve at room temperature. Covered and chilled, this sauce will keep for up to 5 days.

NOTES

⊛ Asian and Indian markets carry excellent tamarind pulp imported from Thailand. Stored airtight at room temperature, it will keep for many months.

⊛ Tamarind pulp is sticky and messy to work with, but its unique, velvety tang will amply reward your trouble. Working the pulp by hand gives the best results, but you can use the back of a large spoon to mash and squeeze it, if you prefer. For more about tamarind pulp, see page 254.

⊛ Tamarind sauce can separate as it sits, so stir gently to restore its thick texture before serving.

APPLE RAISIN CHUTNEY

Makes about 4 cups

THIS CHUTNEY HAS THE DEEP, RICH FLAVOR and luscious texture of homemade jam. My friend Alex makes it in his French farmhouse kitchen in the Loire Valley, using sweet, crisp apples from the orchards that surround his home. I like it with Granny Smiths, but any variety will work well. Apple Raisin Chutney sets off Lamb Curry Kashmiri-Style (page 136).

For a hotter version, add a spicy curry powder or stir in cayenne pepper at the end. This chutney burns easily even at low heat, so be sure to use a heavy pan and stir it well about every 10 minutes once it is simmering, to keep it from sticking.

4 medium apples, about 1 pound (about 4 cups coarsely chopped)	¾ cup cider vinegar
½ cup water	1 cup dark raisins
1 medium onion, finely chopped (about 1 cup)	½ cup light or dark brown sugar
1 tablespoon minced garlic	2 tablespoons curry powder, store-bought or homemade *(page 222, 224 or 226)*
1 can (16-ounce) peeled, chopped tomatoes, including juice (about 2 cups)	2 teaspoons mustard seeds
	½ teaspoon salt

Peel and core the apples, chop them coarsely and place them in a saucepan with the water. Cover, bring to a gentle boil over medium heat and simmer until soft, about 20 minutes.

Meanwhile, combine the onion with the remaining ingredients in a large, heavy saucepan. Stir to mix well.

When the apples are soft, mash them with a fork and add them to the mixture in the large saucepan. Place it on the stove over medium-high heat and bring it to a rolling boil. Stir well, reduce the heat to maintain a simmer, and cook for about 1 hour and 15 minutes. Stir often, scraping the bottom of the pan with a wooden spoon to discourage sticking.

When the chutney is a thick, dark brown, fragrant jam, remove it from the heat and cool to room temperature. Transfer to jars, seal airtight and refrigerate for up to 3 weeks. Serve at room temperature.

NOTE

⊛ Make a double recipe if you want a large batch to share with friends and family. It keeps well and deepens in flavor as it stands.

FRESH MANGO CHUTNEY

Makes 3 cups

THIS GORGEOUS CHUTNEY is a bowl of sunshine on your table, both in its vibrant colors and its extraordinary flavors. It keeps well for several weeks and goes beautifully with grilled and roasted food. While it tastes terrific with any classic curry dish, it is particularly good with Grilled Swordfish Steaks in Cilantro-Ginger Pesto (page 120). Build a vegetarian menu around Fresh Mango Chutney with New Potatoes and Red Bell Peppers in Fresh Green Curry (page 142) and a platter of Basmati Rice (page 163). The recipe comes from my friend Phillis Carey.

2 large, ripe mangoes	¾ cup sugar
1 large apple	½ cup cider vinegar
1 cup finely chopped onion	1½ teaspoons mustard seeds
½ cup diced red bell pepper	1 teaspoon crushed red pepper
½ cup dark raisins	½ teaspoon salt
¼ cup diced crystallized ginger	

Peel the mangoes and cut the fruit into bite-size chunks. Place them in a 3-quart saucepan. Peel and core the apple, chop it coarsely and add it to the saucepan. Add the remaining ingredients and bring to a rolling boil over medium heat. Reduce the heat to low to maintain a gentle simmer, stirring occasionally, until the vegetables are tender and the liquids thicken to a light syrup, 30 to 40 minutes.

Cool to room temperature. Cover and chill until serving time. Bring to room temperature before serving. Covered and refrigerated, the chutney keeps for 3 to 4 weeks.

CUCUMBER RAITA

Makes about 1¼ cups

RAITAS ARE SIMPLE, soothing relishes made of seasoned yogurt and raw vegetables or fruit. Chop, measure, stir and you have it: a cool foil for any curry dish and a sharp, appealing contrast in taste and texture to sweet chutneys, spiced pilafs and warm, rustic breads. This is the quintessential raita, a brisk, refreshing and accessible addition to your curry menu, worth enjoying again and again.

Cucumber Raita complements Jasmine Rice (page 165) and a big bowl of any Thai curry. Served with Green Pea Curry with Fresh Paneer Cheese (page 150), Dal (page 146) and Basmati Rice (page 163), it completes a vegetarian curry supper.

½ teaspoon ground cumin	1 green onion, thinly sliced
½ cup plain yogurt	crosswise
¼ teaspoon salt	1 tablespoon chopped fresh
Freshly ground pepper	cilantro
1 medium cucumber	
(about ½ pound)	

In a small, dry frying pan, toast the cumin over medium heat until fragrant and lightly browned, about 30 seconds. Transfer to a medium bowl and add the yogurt, salt and pepper. Stir well.

Peel the cucumber and cut it in half lengthwise. Using a teaspoon, scoop out the seeds and discard them. Slice the cucumber lengthwise into ½-inch strips and then crosswise to make small cubes. Add to the bowl along with the green onion and cilantro. Stir to combine well. Cover and chill until shortly before serving time.

BANANA RAITA *with* TOASTED COCONUT *and* FRESH MINT

Makes about 1½ cups

THE TANG OF YOGURT sets off the sweetness of banana and toasted coconut in this irresistible cooling relish. This raita is excellent served with Thai Red Curry with Beef, Eggplant and Red Bell Pepper (page 132) and Basmati Rice (page 163), or accompanying Curried Black-Eyed Peas with Eggplant (page 154) and Rice Pilaf with Golden Onions, Cashews and Peas (page 172).

½ cup sweetened flaked or shredded coconut	2 firm, ripe bananas
¾ cup plain yogurt	2 tablespoons finely chopped fresh mint, plus sprigs for garnish
1 tablespoon milk	
¼ teaspoon salt	

In a medium, dry frying pan over high heat, toast the coconut until golden brown, tossing often to even the browning and avoid burning, 2 to 3 minutes. Turn out onto a plate to cool.

In a medium bowl, combine the yogurt, milk and salt and stir well.

Peel the bananas, halve them lengthwise and cut crosswise into ½-inch chunks. Add to the yogurt mixture, along with the chopped mint and the toasted coconut, stirring gently to combine well without bruising the bananas.

Cover and chill 30 minutes or more. Serve cold. Refrigerated, the raita keeps 1 day, though the bananas will soften.

◀◀◀▶▶▶

NOTE

 Peeled bananas and chopped mint keep poorly, so if you are preparing this in advance, combine and chill the yogurt mixture and toast the coconut. Then chop the bananas and mint close to serving time and stir them in.

BEET RAITA

Makes about 1 ¾ cups

AMID THE COMFORTING EARTH TONES on my rice and curry table, this cooling jewel-like dish brings me childlike pleasure with its hot pink color and grown-up satisfaction with its tangy flavor. I enjoy it with Yellow Rice Pilaf with Whole Spices (page 168) and Burmese-Style Pork Curry with Fresh Ginger (page 126).

¾ cup plain yogurt
1 teaspoon peeled, minced fresh
   ginger
1 teaspoon sugar
¼ teaspoon salt

1 can (15-ounce) sliced or
   shredded beets
1 green onion, thinly sliced
   crosswise

In a medium bowl, combine the yogurt, ginger, sugar and salt and stir well.

Drain the beets well and add them to the bowl, along with the green onion. Toss gently to coat the beets with the yogurt mixture. Cover and chill. Serve cold or cool. The raita keeps in the refrigerator for up to 2 days.

TOMATO CUCUMBER RELISH

Makes about 1¾ cups

THE CLEAR FLAVORS AND VIBRANT COLORS of this dish suggest the fresh tomato salsas of Mexico, so finely chop all the ingredients if you want a sprightly dip to serve with tortilla chips. Add thin slices of serrano chili pepper if you want.

4   plum tomatoes
½   medium cucumber
¾   cup finely chopped onion
2   tablespoons chopped fresh
      cilantro, plus sprigs for
      garnish

2   tablespoons freshly squeezed
      lime juice
½   teaspoon salt

Remove the stem ends of the tomatoes and discard. Halve the tomatoes lengthwise, then slice them crosswise into small chunks. Transfer to a medium bowl.

Peel the cucumber and remove the ends. Halve the cucumber lengthwise, scoop out and discard the seeds, then cut it lengthwise into strips and crosswise into small chunks. Add to the bowl with the tomatoes.

Add the onion, chopped cilantro, lime juice and salt and stir to combine well. Cover and chill for 30 minutes. Serve cold or cool, garnished with sprigs of fresh cilantro. The relish keeps 2 days, covered and chilled.

SWEET *and* SOUR CUCUMBER SALAD

Makes about 1¼ cups

THIS RELISH is an ideal accompaniment to any curry. It counterpoints the fire and sweetness of Thailand's coconut-milk curries and is the traditional accompaniment to satay with peanut sauce. Like the refrigerator pickles of my Southern childhood, it is a good thing to have on hand no matter what is on the menu.

½ cup white vinegar	¼ cup coarsely chopped red onion
½ cup water	2 tablespoons coarsely chopped
½ cup sugar	fresh cilantro, plus sprigs
1 teaspoon salt	for garnish
1 large cucumber	2 tablespoons finely chopped
(about ¾ pound)	dry-roasted peanuts

In a small saucepan, combine the vinegar, water, sugar and salt over medium heat and bring to a gentle boil, stirring occasionally to dissolve the sugar and salt. When the syrup is clear and slightly thickened, about 2 minutes, remove from the heat and let it cool to room temperature.

Peel the cucumber and quarter it lengthwise, to make 4 long strips. Slice the strips crosswise into little triangles about ¼ inch thick. In a medium bowl, combine the cucumber with the dressing, onion and chopped cilantro and stir well.

To serve, scoop the cucumber out of the dressing and into a serving bowl, using a slotted spoon. Add some dressing, sprinkle the peanuts on top and add a small handful of cilantro leaves.

◀◀◀◀ ▶▶▶▶

NOTES

⊛ If you have tender cucumbers from the garden or hothouse cucumbers with nice, unwaxed skin, leave some of the skin on. If you are using a large seedy cucumber, halve it lengthwise, scoop out and discard the seeds with a spoon, and cut each half crosswise into moon-shaped slices.

⊛ I prefer these pickles crisp, so when preparing them in advance, I mix the cucumbers into the chilled dressing about 1 hour before serving. But it is fine to make them up completely in advance, stirring in the peanuts and cilantro leaves, and to keep them covered and chilled for 2 to 3 days.

FRESH LEMONGRASS COOLER

Serves 5

L EMONGRASS IS EASY TO GROW (see page 251), and an extra reward for your trouble is the chance to enjoy this unusual, refreshing drink made from the delicate-tasting spearlike leaves.

I learned the recipe at Takrai Restaurant in the northern Thai city of Chiang Mai. *Takrai* is the Thai word for lemongrass, and the dining room is graced with huge pots of the namesake herb.

¼ cup water	3 cups cold water
¼ cup sugar	Ice cubes
Leaves from 3-5 fresh lemongrass stalks	

In a small saucepan over high heat, combine the ¼ cup water and sugar. Stir frequently, heating just until the sugar is dissolved and the water is clear, about 2 minutes. Transfer to a blender.

Using kitchen scissors, hold a few lemongrass leaves at a time over a large bowl and cut them crosswise into 2-inch lengths. Or use a sharp knife, placing a few leaves at a time on your cutting board and cutting them crosswise into 2-inch strips. Measure out about 2 cups of the leaves, loosely packed. Add the leaves to the blender, along with the 3 cups cold water.

Blend at high speed for 1 to 2 minutes, stopping occasionally to stir up the leaves from around the blade. When the water is bright green and foamy and the leaves are shredded into fine, sharp pieces, strain the liquid through a fine sieve into a large bowl or pitcher. Scoop off the foam with a spoon and discard it.

Serve in a tall glass over ice. Chilled, the cooler will keep for 1 to 2 days, but it tastes best freshly made.

◀◀◀ ▶▶▶

NOTE

✹ If you have an abundance of lemongrass leaves, cut up any extra ones, as directed, into 2-inch lengths, place in a self-sealing plastic bag, press out as much air as possible and seal. Freeze for up to 6 weeks. To use in this recipe, add to the blender without defrosting, and use an extra cup of frozen leaves to boost the flavor after freezing.

LAHSSIE

Makes about 1½ cups; 1 large or 2 small servings

THIS TRADITIONAL BEVERAGE is an extraordinarily refreshing drink, as the prelude to a five-alarm curry feast, as part of a busy morning's quick breakfast on the run or as a cooling pick-me-up on a sultry afternoon. If you can find rose water at an Indian market, add a spoonful to the blender along with the sugar.

1 cup plain yogurt	1 tablespoon light or
2 ice cubes	dark brown sugar

In a blender, combine the yogurt, ice cubes and brown sugar and blend until smooth, using short pulses to crush the ice cubes.

Transfer to a tall glass and serve at once.

NOTE

⊛ This keeps well for up to a day. It will separate as it sits, so stir well or put it back in the blender before serving.

Mango Yogurt Smoothie

Makes 2½ cups; serves 2 or 3

THE SUNRISE COLOR OF THIS COOLER makes it a pleasure to look at as well as to drink. Try it with fresh peaches or nectarines when ripe mangoes are hard to find.

1	large, ripe mango (about 1 pound)	4	ice cubes
½	cup water	1	tablespoon light or dark brown sugar
1	cup plain yogurt	¼	teaspoon ground cinnamon

Peel the mango and hold it in the palm of your hand. Cutting away from you with a long, sharp knife, pare the fruit from the large seed at the center, turning to expose as much fruit as possible to the blade without including the fibrous portions close to the seed. Chop the fruit into large chunks. You should have about 2 cups.

In a blender, combine the water, yogurt, ice cubes, brown sugar, cinnamon and mango. Blend at high speed until smooth, using short pulses to crush the ice cubes.

Transfer to glasses and serve at once.

CHAPTER 8

CURRY PASTES, CURRY POWDERS AND OTHER BASIC RECIPES

THIS CHAPTER IS FOR THOSE who enjoy the challenges of cooking from scratch. You may want to make your own curry pastes and powders because commercial varieties lack the freshness and personal touch of those you can create in your own kitchen. Or you may live far from an Indian or Asian market and find it essential to make your own curry components. Whatever your reason, if your schedule allows, you will reap a precious harvest for taking the time and energy to gather the spices, prepare them and grind them at home. Although you can grind them just before you stir them into a dish, it's best to schedule those sessions for a time when you have an hour or so to devote to this task.

Having dry-fried the whole spices and chopped the herbal components of their curry pastes into bits, Thai cooks lay everything out on a big tray and repair to a pleasing spot on a straw mat on the veranda. There they can sit and snack and work and visit, passing the time as they pound away and scrape down the sides of the mortar's bowl, coaxing everything into the wet, fragrant essence. I have been known to set up shop on a big, old quilt by the fireplace, with a mug of tea and my mortar, pestle and tray of ingredients before me, and a vintage Joni Mitchell on the stereo to keep me company.

BEFORE BEING GROUND, however, the spices must be toasted to enhance and deepen their flavor and to make them easier to digest. There are three basic methods of toasting spices.

Toasting Whole Spices on the Stovetop

The first method is to start with whole spices, toast them, one by one, on top of the stove, and then grind them to a fine powder once they have cooled. Toasting whole spices is preferable to toasting ground ones, because whole spices retain their flavor for a longer time. Ground spices begin to deteriorate in flavor as soon as they are ground and continue to lose intensity the longer they

stand. They also burn faster, making it impossible to toast them long enough to develop the maximum flavor.

Each whole spice needs its own toasting session, and you must use your eyes and nose to guide you in deciding when a given spice is handsomely darkened and enhanced in fragrance without being burned. This is the traditional method in India, Thailand and other Southeast Asian countries. You will use this method for Sri Lankan-Style Curry Powder (page 226).

I use a small, dry, nonstick frying pan and work over medium heat, shaking the pan or stirring often and keeping my full attention on the spices, which can go from fragrant to scorched within seconds. If you are eager to get the job done and confident about the process, you can toast over higher heat for a shorter period of time.

Toasting times will vary among different spices, with cumin smoking and burning in the time it would take coriander to fully develop its color and flavor. Note that the spices will continue to darken briefly once they are off the heat, and should be removed from the stove just before they reach the depth of color you want.

Toasting Whole Spices in the Oven

The second method is to toast various whole spices together in a moderate oven, spreading them out on a baking sheet and stirring occasionally to expose them evenly to the heat. This method takes a bit longer and denies you the pleasure of watching the process. But it frees you to relax or handle another task or two, and your kitchen will be filled with a lovely perfume. Since the process is slower with gentler heat, there is no problem in toasting all the whole spices together at one time. You will use this method in the recipes for Basic Curry Powder (page 222) and for Garam Masala, Roasted and Savory (page 230).

Toasting Ground Spices

The third method is to use ground spices, combining them all and toasting them briefly in a small, dry frying pan on top of the stove. They will toast quickly, so pay very close attention to your work and keep them moving almost constantly. Some spices, such as turmeric and paprika, are seldom toasted, as their presence in curry pastes and powders is to provide color rather than flavor. You will toast ground spices in the recipes for Easy Curry Powder (page 224) and for all four Thai-style curry pastes (page 214 to 220). If you would like extra flavor for a little extra effort, you could use whole cumin and coriander seeds in the Thai curry pastes, toasting each spice separately on top of the stove and then grinding them together to a fine powder when they have cooled.

Grinding Spices

There are two ways of grinding whole spices for curry powder and pastes. To grind small spices, such as whole cumin, coriander and peppercorns, you can use a coffee grinder that you keep expressly for the purpose. If you also use it for grinding coffee, it will season the beans henceforth in a novel but probably un-appealing way. Large spices, such as cinnamon sticks and nutmeg, will need to be crushed to pieces separately before being added to the coffee grinder or, in the case of nutmeg, grated and stirred together with the other spices after grinding.

Alternatively, you can use a large, heavy Thai-style mortar and pestle. Check the equipment section of Asian markets for these extraordinary and beautiful pieces of ancient kitchen equipment, or see page 257 for a mail-order source. They are indispensable tools if you want to make curry pastes in the traditional manner. Their large capacity and heft make them useful for grinding hard spices and sturdy herbs, such as lemongrass and galanga, in a way that the more delicate European mortars and pestles could never match.

Your first choice should be a mortar made of granite or other stone, with a matching stone pestle. Your second choice should be a crockery mortar with a wooden pestle. These Lao-style mortars are generally taller and deeper, as they are used for pounding up green papaya salad and other dishes, as well as for grinding spices, curry pastes, sauces and traditional medicines.

If you want to grind your own curry pastes with greater speed and less elbow grease, use a blender or a mini food processor. In a blender, you will need to add water or another liquid to keep the blades moving enough to grind everything together well. In a mini food processor, you may not need liquid but you may need to grind your curry paste in batches, as these machines tend to have a small capacity. I prefer mini food processors to large ones when grinding curry pastes, because the large machines leave the fibrous ingredients, such as lemongrass and galanga, in large chunks—undesirable both in curry paste and in a curry dish.

Personally, I find many of the pre-pared curry powders and pastes on the market to be welcome additions to my kitchen, enabling me to enjoy curries and curry-flavored dishes far more often than I could possibly do if I made everything from scratch every time. But when

I have a day to seek out the ingredients and chop, toast and grind up my garam masala or Thai-style green curry paste at home, I enjoy both the process and the superb results. I find that what I make is worth the effort, serving me and my guests long after the sometimes laborious process of making them becomes a memory.

IN ADDITION TO RECIPES for curry powders and pastes, this chapter will provide recipes for several other ingredients called for in this cookbook that are difficult and sometimes impossible to find. Ghee is the traditional Indian version of clarified butter, used to fry onions and add a luxurious depth of flavor to many curries and pilafs. Paneer cheese is a simple, mild-flavored cheese used in vegetarian dishes, including the green pea curry called *mattar paneer*. Tamarind liquid is extracted from the fruit of the tamarind tree, providing a smoky, sweet-and-sour flavor to dishes of Indian and Southeast Asian origin. Cashew milk and other nut milks provide a deliciously creamy alternative to dairy milk and cream for vegan cooks. Sweet and Spicy Garlic Sauce is a terrific Thai-style dipping sauce you will want to keep on hand to serve with grilled chicken or vegetables, as well as with crisp-fried tidbits such as Curried Fresh Corn Fritters.

Curry Pastes, Curry Powders
and Other Basic Recipes

Green Curry Paste Thai-Style

Makes about ¾ cup

GREEN CURRY PASTE takes its name from the fresh green chili peppers that create its heat. If you can find wild lime leaves in an Asian market, chop up half a dozen and add them to your curry paste for an extra burst of Southeast Asian flavor and perfume. If you want a hotter green curry paste, increase the amount of fresh hot green chilies to as much as ½ cup. For a milder paste, decrease the amount of fresh hot green chilies to 1 or 2 tablespoons.

1 tablespoon ground coriander
1 teaspoon ground cumin
1 teaspoon salt
½ teaspoon freshly ground pepper
¼ cup coarsely chopped fresh hot green chili peppers, such as serrano, jalapeño or Thai prik kii noo
¼ cup coarsely chopped fresh cilantro, including stems, leaves and roots, if available

¼ cup coarsely chopped shallots
3 tablespoons coarsely chopped garlic
3 tablespoons minced fresh lemongrass (about 3 stalks); *see Notes*
1 tablespoon minced fresh galanga *(page 249)* or fresh ginger
1 teaspoon grated fresh lime zest
Few tablespoons water

Place a small plate by the stove to hold the spices. Combine the coriander and cumin in a small, dry frying pan. Place over medium heat and toast the spices 1 to 2 minutes, stirring often, until fragrant and slightly darkened. Remove from the heat and tip out onto the plate. Add the salt and pepper and set aside.

In a blender or mini food processor, combine the chilies, cilantro, shallots, garlic, lemongrass, galanga or ginger, lime zest, 2 tablespoons water and spices. Process to a fairly smooth, evenly colored paste, stopping often to scrape down the sides and grind everything well. Add a little more water as needed to keep the blades moving.

Transfer the curry paste to a jar and seal airtight. Refrigerate for up to 1 month.

NOTES

❀ To prepare the lemongrass, trim each stalk to about 3 inches in length, including the bulbous base. Trim away any dried, hard portion at the root end and discard any dried outer leaves. Chop the trimmed stalks coarsely and finely grind them in a mini food processor. To prepare by hand, cut each trimmed stalk crosswise into very thin slices and mince.

❀ Thais put cilantro root in curry pastes for moisture and a mild herbaceous boost. Use the white root portion along with about 1 inch of the lower stem. Chopped stems and leaves make a good substitute.

❀ For a more traditional version, use equal amounts of whole cumin and coriander seeds, toasting them separately over medium heat, shaking the pan often, until fragrant and a few shades darker. Cumin takes only 2 to 3 minutes, while coriander takes 4 to 5. Keep some of each of the raw spices handy by the stove, to help you judge the color change as you are toasting. Grind to a powder, using a spice grinder, a coffee grinder kept especially for that purpose or a mortar.

❀ This paste freezes well for up to 6 months. Consider freezing in tablespoon-size portions if you plan to defrost just enough for one curry.

Yellow Curry Paste Thai-Style

Makes about ½ cup

IN THAILAND, yellow curry paste is simply red curry paste colored with a sunny splash of fresh or ground turmeric. Turmeric is the most colorful member of the ginger family, treasured throughout Asia for its medicinal properties as well as for its gorgeous golden hue. Yellow curry paste has less chili-fueled fire than red curry paste and is often saved for shrimp, fish or other seafood.

For a more traditional version, use whole coriander and cumin seeds; see page 215.

10 small dried red chili peppers *(see Notes)*	¼ cup chopped garlic
1 tablespoon ground coriander	3 tablespoons minced fresh lemongrass (about 3 stalks); *page 215*
1 tablespoon ground cumin	
1 teaspoon ground turmeric	1 tablespoon minced fresh galanga *(page 249)* or fresh ginger
1 teaspoon salt	
½ teaspoon ground cinnamon	
¼ teaspoon freshly ground pepper	Few tablespoons water
¼ cup chopped shallots	

Stem the chilies and cut them into small pieces, using kitchen scissors or a knife. Place in a small bowl and add warm water to cover. Let them soak for about 15 minutes until softened. Drain and set aside.

Meanwhile, place a small plate by the stove to hold the spices. Combine the coriander and cumin in a small, dry frying pan. Place over medium heat and toast the spices 1 to 2 minutes, stirring often, until fragrant and slightly darkened. Remove from the heat and tip out onto the plate. Add the turmeric, salt, cinnamon and pepper and set aside.

In a blender or mini food processor, combine the shallots, garlic, lemongrass, galanga or ginger, 2 tablespoons water, drained chilies and spices. Process to a fairly smooth, evenly colored paste, stopping often to scrape down the sides and grind everything well. Add water as needed to keep the blades moving.

Transfer the curry paste to a jar and seal airtight. Refrigerate until needed for up to 1 month.

NOTES

⊛ Many grocery stores carry spices and dried herbs for Mexican cooking, and this is where you can find excellent dried red chili peppers. Look for *chiles Japones* or *chiles de arbol,* which are slender chilies a bit longer and thinner than your pinkie finger. Or check Asian, Indian and other ethnic markets for a wide array. Use about a tablespoon of chopped dried red chili if you are using a larger variety than these.

⊛ This paste freezes well for up to 6 months. Consider freezing in tablespoon-size portions if you plan to defrost just enough for one curry at a time.

RED CURRY PASTE THAI-STYLE

Makes about ¾ cup

RED CURRY PASTE is named for the deep rust color of its dried red chilies. Using about ¼ cup of any hot dried red chili, measured after it is stemmed and chopped, will give you a hot, Thai-style curry paste. You can crank the heat up or down by increasing or decreasing the amount of chilies you use. If you decrease the amount of hot chilies, you may want to add some paprika to lend color to your curry. For a more traditional version, use whole coriander and cumin seeds; see page 215.

15 small dried red chili peppers *(page 217)*	3 tablespoons minced fresh lemongrass (3-4 stalks); *page 215*
1 tablespoon ground coriander	3 tablespoons coarsely chopped fresh cilantro stems and leaves
1½ teaspoons ground cumin	
1 teaspoon salt	1 heaping tablespoon coarsely chopped fresh galanga *(page 249)* or fresh ginger
½ teaspoon freshly ground pepper	
¼ cup coarsely chopped shallots (3-4)	
3 tablespoons coarsely chopped garlic	1 teaspoon grated fresh lime zest Few tablespoons water

Stem the chilies and cut into small pieces, using kitchen scissors or a knife. There should be about ¼ cup. Place in a small bowl and add warm water to cover. Let them soak for about 15 minutes until softened. Drain and set aside.

Meanwhile, place a small plate by the stove to hold the spices. Combine the coriander and cumin in a small, dry frying pan. Place over medium heat and toast the spices 1 to 2 minutes, stirring often, until fragrant and slightly darkened. Remove from the heat and tip out onto the plate. Add the salt and pepper and set aside.

In a blender or mini food processor, combine the shallots, garlic, lemongrass, cilantro, galanga or ginger, lime zest, 2 tablespoons water, drained chilies and spices. Process to a fairly smooth, evenly colored paste, stopping often to scrape down the sides and grind everything well. Add a little more water as needed to keep the blades moving.

Transfer the curry paste to a jar and seal airtight. Refrigerate until needed for up to 1 month.

NOTE

⊛ This paste freezes well for up to 6 months. Consider freezing in tablespoon-size portions if you plan to defrost just enough for one curry at a time.

MUSSAMUN CURRY PASTE THAI-STYLE

Makes about 1 cup

THIS CURRY PASTE offers a cornucopia of sweet spices set against a moderate fire created by hot red chilies. In Thailand, mussamun curries are often served as part of a feast hosted by families celebrating a wedding, a move to a new home, the birth of a baby or the ordination of a son as a Buddhist monk. The classic mussamun version pairs chunks of beef or chicken (page 105) with potatoes, peanuts and whole cardamom pods, an unusual combination that reflects the distant Indian Muslim origins of a dish adopted and adapted by Thai cooks many years ago.

15	small dried red chili peppers *(page 217)*	2	teaspoons salt
2	teaspoons ground cumin	½	cup coarsely chopped onion
1	teaspoon ground coriander	½	cup chopped garlic
1	teaspoon freshly ground pepper	3	tablespoons minced fresh lemongrass (about 3 stalks); *page 215*
1	teaspoon ground cinnamon		
1	teaspoon ground nutmeg	1	tablespoon minced fresh galanga *(page 249)* or fresh ginger
1	teaspoon ground cardamom		
½	teaspoon ground cloves		
½	teaspoon ground turmeric		Few tablespoons water

Stem the chilies and cut them into small pieces, using kitchen scissors or a knife. There should be about ¼ cup. Place in a small bowl and add warm water to cover. Let them soak for about 15 minutes until softened. Drain and set aside.

Meanwhile, place a small plate by the stove to hold the spices. Combine the cumin and coriander in a small, dry frying pan. Place over medium heat and toast the spices 1 to 2 minutes, stirring often, until fragrant and slightly darkened. Remove from the heat and tip out onto the plate. Add the pepper, cinnamon, nutmeg, cardamom, cloves, turmeric and salt and set aside.

In a blender or mini food processor, combine the onion, garlic, lemongrass, galanga or ginger, 2 tablespoons water, drained chilies and spices. Process to a fairly smooth, evenly colored paste, stopping often to scrape down the sides and grind everything well. Add a little more water as needed to keep the blades moving.

Transfer the curry paste to a jar and seal airtight. Refrigerate until needed for up to 1 month.

NOTE

⊗ This paste can be frozen for up to 6 months. Consider freezing in tablespoon-size portions if you plan to defrost just enough for one curry at a time.

BASIC CURRY POWDER

Makes about ¾ cup

THIS IS MY VERSION of the standard spice mixture known as curry powder. Use it as is, or play with the basic combination as you wish. You may want to vary the proportions of spices given, omit some or add any of the following: fennel seeds, star anise, ground nutmeg or mace, dried curry leaves or brown or black mustard seeds. You can substitute ground spices if you keep in mind that they burn quickly and should be toasted separately. (See Notes for advice on adapting this recipe with ground spices.)

¼ cup coriander seeds

2 tablespoons cumin seeds

1 tablespoon white or black peppercorns

2 teaspoons fenugreek seeds

2 cinnamon sticks, each about 3 inches long

1 tablespoon ground turmeric

2 teaspoons whole cardamom seeds or ground cardamom

1 teaspoon whole cloves

1 teaspoon ground ginger

1 dried red chili pepper, stemmed and broken into small pieces, or 2 teaspoons coarsely ground dried red chilies or ¼ teaspoon ground cayenne pepper

Preheat the oven to 300 degrees F.

In a pie tin or cake pan, combine the coriander, cumin, peppercorns and fenugreek. Wrap the cinnamon sticks in a kitchen towel and crush them with a rolling pin or the side of an unopened can. Add the crushed cinnamon to the pan of spices and place it in the oven.

Toast the spices for 15 minutes, stirring once, until they darken a little and release their flavors. Remove from the oven and transfer to a plate to cool to room temperature.

Meanwhile, combine the turmeric, cardamom, cloves, ginger and chili pepper or cayenne on another plate. When the toasted spices have cooled, combine them with the untoasted spices and grind to a fine powder in a spice grinder, a coffee grinder reserved for that purpose or a mortar. Transfer to a jar, seal airtight and store away from heat and light. Use within 3 months.

NOTES

✸ Keep some of each of the raw spices handy by the stove, to help you judge the color change as you are toasting.

✸ For ground spices, use the same amount as for whole spices. You will need 1 teaspoon ground cinnamon. Combine any ground spices that need to be toasted—coriander, cumin, pepper and fenugreek, if you can find it ground—in a small, dry frying pan and toast over medium heat 1 to 2 minutes, until fragrant and slightly darkened, stirring often. Set aside to cool, combine with the other spices and continue as directed.

EASY CURRY POWDER

Makes about ½ cup

THIS CURRY POWDER is made with an accessible array of spices found in most grocery stores. Using ground spices simplifies toasting and eliminates the step of grinding. But take care, since ground spices burn more quickly. If they char, toss them out the back door and start again.

3	tablespoons ground coriander	2	teaspoons ground cinnamon
2	tablespoons ground cumin	2	teaspoons ground ginger
2	teaspoons freshly ground pepper	2	teaspoons ground cardamom
		1	teaspoon ground cayenne
2	teaspoons ground cloves	2	tablespoons ground turmeric

Measure all the spices except the turmeric into a medium, dry frying pan and stir to combine them well. Have a plate handy next to the stove on which to cool the spices.

Place the frying pan over medium heat and toast, stirring constantly, until the spices darken a little and release their fragrance, about 3 minutes. Wisps of smoke will rise up from the pan as the spices toast. Tip them out onto the plate to cool to room temperature. Add the turmeric and stir with a fork or small whisk until the spice powder is evenly colored. Seal airtight and store away from heat and light. Use within 3 months.

NOTES

❋ A funnel helps transfer a quantity of spice powder to a jar without spilling.

❋ Choose a large-mouth jar so it's easy to put in a tablespoon for measuring.

SRI LANKAN-STYLE CURRY POWDER

Makes about ⅔ cup

IN SRI LANKA, CURRIES TEND TO BE VERY HOT, with a deep, rich flavor that comes from toasting the spices before grinding.

20	whole cardamom pods or	2	teaspoons peppercorns
	1 teaspoon cardamom seeds	2	cinnamon sticks, each about
10	whole cloves		3 inches long, broken
3	tablespoons coriander seeds		into pieces
2	tablespoons cumin seeds	2	teaspoons dried red
1	tablespoon fennel seeds		pepper flakes
2	teaspoons fenugreek seeds	1	tablespoon ground turmeric

Measure out each spice into its own small bowl, except the turmeric, which does not need toasting. If using whole cardamom pods, remove the husks by placing the pods in a spice grinder or coffee grinder reserved for that purpose or a mortar and pulse or pound for about 10 seconds, until the pods open and release most of their seeds. Next to the stove, set a large plate on which the spices will cool. In a medium, dry frying pan over medium-high heat, toast the spices, one by one, until fragrant and a shade or two darker. Transfer each spice to the plate as soon as it is done.

When cool, grind the spices to a fine powder in a spice grinder, coffee grinder or a mortar. Transfer to a medium bowl, stir in the turmeric and mix well. Store airtight, away from heat and light. Use within 3 months.

NOTES

⊛ Keep some of each raw spice handy by the stove, to help you judge the color change as you are toasting.

⊛ You can substitute ground spices whenever possible, though it is likely you will have to work with whole fennel and fenugreek, as they are seldom available ground.

GARAM MASALA, UNROASTED *and* SWEET

Makes about ½ cup

THIS CLASSIC MIXTURE OF GROUND SPICES is used often in Indian cooking to season food as it cooks. It is also sprinkled over many dishes just before they are served, to set off a pleasing explosion of flavor and a cloud of spicy perfume. In the Hindi language, *masala* means a particular combination of herbs and spices. *Garam* means warming and refers not to the heat we associate with chili peppers and peppercorns but to ancient Hindu teachings about health. Many traditional Indian cooks believe that certain foods have heating or cooling effects on the body. Cardamom, cinnamon, peppercorns and cloves, common to most versions of garam masala, are among the spices that are considered warming.

Recipes for garam masala are many, varying by region, over the course of time and from cook to cook. This is not surprising in a land where the ability to cook well and season food imaginatively is a source of pride and cause for respect. This classic version is based on a traditional formula of these four warming spices in equal portions by weight. This mixture is unroasted, to make the most of the fact that these spices are profoundly aromatic and pungent in their natural state. You can use either this recipe or the one on page 230 in any dish calling for garam masala. I prefer this one because it is the simplest.

⅓ cup black or green
　　cardamom pods
5 cinnamon sticks, each about
　　3 inches long

¼ cup whole cloves
2 tablespoons plus 2 teaspoons
　　black peppercorns

To remove the husks from the cardamom pods, place the whole pods in a spice grinder, coffee grinder reserved for that purpose or a mortar and pulse or pound for about 10 seconds, until the pods open and release most of their seeds. Shake out any remaining seeds and discard the pods.

Break the cinnamon sticks into pieces by hand or by wrapping in a clean kitchen towel and pounding lightly with the side of an unopened can, a mallet or rolling pin. Grind the cardamom seeds, broken cinnamon sticks, cloves and peppercorns to a fine powder in a spice grinder, coffee grinder or mortar. Store airtight away from heat and light. Use within 3 months.

NOTE

✹ You can substitute ground spices here, combining 2 tablespoons each ground cardamom, cinnamon, cloves and black pepper, stirring well to blend them until each spice disappears into the mixture. If possible, use freshly ground pepper.

GARAM MASALA, ROASTED *and* SAVORY

Makes about ⅔ cup

LIKE THE PREVIOUS RECIPE, this is my version of the classic spice mixture known as *garam masala*. Here the spices are roasted in the oven to deepen their flavor before they are ground to a powder, which will keep several months. This mixture has a more complex flavor and is the more common of the two garam masalas. Either one will work well in any dish calling for this classic Indian spice mixture.

⅓ cup green cardamom pods	2 tablespoons plus 2 teaspoons black peppercorns
5 cinnamon sticks, each about 3 inches long	2 teaspoons cumin seeds
¼ (scant) cup whole cloves	1 teaspoon coriander seeds
	½ teaspoon freshly grated nutmeg

Preheat the oven to 300 degrees F.

To remove the husks from the cardamom pods, place them in a spice grinder, coffee grinder reserved for that purpose or a mortar and pulse or pound for about 10 seconds, until the pods open and release most of their seeds. Shake out any remaining seeds and discard the pods.

Break the cinnamon into pieces by hand, or by wrapping in a clean kitchen towel and pounding lightly with the side of an unopened can, a mallet or rolling pin. Shake the cinnamon out onto a baking pan and add the cardamom seeds, cloves, peppercorns, cumin and coriander.

Place the baking pan in the oven and roast the spices for 15 minutes, stirring once, until fragrant and a shade or two darker. Remove and cool to room temperature, transfer to a spice grinder, coffee grinder or mortar and grind to a fine powder. Add the nutmeg and grind again briefly. Transfer to a small jar and seal airtight. Store away from heat and light. Use within 3 months.

◀◀◀▶▶▶

NOTES

⊛ Keep some of each of the raw spices handy by the stove, to help you judge the color change as you are roasting.

⊛ You can substitute ground spices for whole spices in this recipe with very good results. In a small bowl combine the following spices:

3½ tablespoons ground cardamom	2 teaspoons ground cumin
2½ tablespoons ground cinnamon	1½ teaspoons ground coriander
¼ cup ground cloves	½ teaspoon freshly grated nutmeg
¼ cup freshly ground black pepper	**(do not roast with other spices)**

Stir all the spices, except the nutmeg, together to combine well. Tip them into a medium, dry frying pan and place it over medium heat. Roast, stirring almost constantly, for about 3 minutes, until they release wisps of fragrant smoke and turn a few shades darker but not black. Reserve a bit of the unroasted mixture on a saucer by the stove to help you judge the color change. Tip out onto a plate to cool. Stir in the nutmeg, transfer to an airtight jar and store away from heat and light. Use within 3 months.

SWEET and SPICY GARLIC SAUCE

Makes about 1 cup

IN THAILAND, this dipping sauce brings sweet, sour and fiery notes to spring rolls, crab cakes and Thai Grilled Chicken (page 96). Use it for a delicious accent to any crisp fried tidbit or whatever is hot off the grill. It is easy and keeps beautifully. Make it in advance, as it needs about a half hour to cook, plus time to cool to room temperature.

1 cup sugar	1 teaspoon salt
½ cup white vinegar	1 tablespoon chili garlic sauce
½ cup water	*(page 243)* or coarsely ground
2 tablespoons minced garlic	dried red chili peppers

In a medium saucepan, combine the sugar, vinegar, water, garlic and salt and stir well. Place over medium-high heat and bring to a rolling boil. Stir well, reduce the heat to maintain a gentle, active boil, and cook 30 minutes, until thickened to a clear, slightly golden syrup, thicker than maple syrup but thinner than honey. Remove from the heat, stir in the chili garlic sauce or dried red chilies and cool to room temperature.

Serve at room temperature as a dipping sauce with grilled and fried foods. This sauce thickens as it stands, so dilute it as needed, adding 2 tablespoons water and stirring often as you warm it over medium heat. The sauce keeps refrigerated for 2 to 3 days.

CASHEW MILK

Makes 2¼ cups

USE THIS CREAMY NONDAIRY BASE in soups and stews in place of milk, coconut milk or light cream. You can substitute pine nuts, almonds or pecans for the cashews. Choose raw or roasted nuts, keeping in mind that roasted will impart a stronger nutty flavor.

2 cups water or chicken or vegetable broth

1 cup cashews, either raw or roasted, preferably unsalted (*see Note*)

In a blender, combine the water or broth with the cashews and blend for 2 minutes, scraping down the sides occasionally, until you have a smooth, rich milk. Use immediately or transfer to an airtight jar and refrigerate for 3 to 5 days.

◀◀◀▶▶▶

NOTE

Salted cashews will work if you remember to adjust the salt in recipes in which you use the cashew milk, tasting first and adding salt only as needed.

GHEE

Makes about 6 tablespoons, a generous ⅓ cup

THIS ANCIENT RECIPE calls for melting butter slowly over very low heat. The water evaporates while the milk solids separate. The foamy crust that forms on top of the melted butter is then skimmed off. What is left after straining is pure butterfat, the clear golden liquid known in the Hindi language as *ghee*.

Ghee can be used for long, slow frying, for it does not burn quickly as butter would, and it keeps well at room temperature for months in tropical kitchens. As it turns from butter into ghee, its flavor is transformed to toasted nutty heights, enhancing the dishes in which it is used.

Even when the butter is cooked on low heat, a heavy saucepan is essential to avoid burning. This makes about 6 tablespoons, enough for you to try in a recipe or two. For a larger supply, use more butter in a larger pan.

8   tablespoons (½ cup) unsalted butter

In a small, heavy saucepan over very low heat, allow the butter to melt undisturbed. Within 5 to 10 minutes, the butter will bubble and crackle and release a little steam, and a layer of white foam will form on the top. Let the butter gently cook for a total of about 45 minutes, without stirring. It will cook down somewhat during this time.

Remove from the heat and carefully skim off and discard the crusty top layer, which looks like a soft topping of bread crumbs. Slowly pour most of the ghee through a very fine mesh strainer or several layers of cheesecloth into a small bowl, taking care to leave behind any foam from the top or darkened solids that may have settled to the bottom. The ghee will be a clear, lemon-yellow essence.

Transfer the strained ghee to a jar and seal airtight. Store in a cool, dark place or refrigerate until needed for up to 1 month.

◀◀◀◀▶▶▶▶

NOTES

❀ To make larger quantities of ghee: Use 1 cup (2 sticks) unsalted butter for about 1½ cups ghee, and 1½ cups (3 sticks) unsalted butter for about 2¼ cups ghee.

❀ Ghee often thickens as it stands at room temperature, so do not be concerned if your clear golden ghee turns to a thick, cloudy yellow puree after it cools. It cooks the same and will melt as you heat it for your recipe.

❀ While ghee is traditionally kept at room temperature, you may keep it refrigerated if you prefer.

❀ For a mail-order source for ghee, see pages 257 to 259.

PANEER CHEESE

Makes about 8 ounces,
or about 2 cups of loosely packed ½-inch cubes

PANEER IS A SIMPLE, MILD-FLAVORED INDIAN CHEESE that is commercially unavailable in the West but easy to make at home. Once you try this, you will have a new appreciation for the Little Miss Muffet nursery rhyme, for you will know the meaning of curds and whey. More importantly, you will be able to enjoy my version of the lovely Indian dish called *mattar paneer*, a simple, delicious vegetarian curry made with green peas, tomatoes, curry spices and your own fresh paneer cheese (page 150). Consider making a double batch if you like this simple, homey cheese as much as I do.

6 cups whole milk	1½ cups plain whole-milk yogurt

Prepare a place for the paneer to drain, placing a colander in the sink and lining it with 4 thicknesses of cheesecloth or a clean linen kitchen towel.

In a large (at least 3-quart) saucepan, bring the milk to a boil over high heat, stirring almost constantly to prevent it from burning or boiling over. As soon as the milk comes to the boil, add the yogurt and stir gently. The milk will soon foam up into soft clouds and then break into thick curds of cheese floating in a thin, faintly greenish liquid called whey.

Remove from the heat and pour the contents of the saucepan into the cheesecloth-lined colander placed in the sink, to drain away the whey. When the cloth is cool enough to handle, bring its corners together and squeeze the cheese into a ball, twisting the top portion of the cloth to force out more liquid and then securing it with a rubber band.

Suspend the cheese from the faucet and let it hang over the sink for about 30 minutes, to drain off any remaining whey.

Now press the cheese to make it firm enough to cut. Place the wrapped lump of cheese on its side in a pie pan or frying pan, and place another pie pan or frying pan of equal or smaller size on top of it, or cover the cheese with a plate. Balance a weighty object, such as a teakettle filled with water, on the pan or plate to compress the cheese. Press for 30 minutes more.

Carefully unwrap the pressed cheese, cut into ½-inch cubes, transfer it to a container and seal airtight. Refrigerate until needed. The paneer will keep 3 to 4 days in the refrigerator and several months in the freezer.

NOTES

⊛ When the milk comes to a boil, it will bubble up and foam as the cheese is formed, so it needs lots of room. To avoid spills, use a large, deep saucepan to contain it.

⊛ Another traditional way of making paneer uses lemon juice instead of yogurt. I prefer yogurt because the yield is larger. To use lemon juice with 6 cups milk, add 3 to 4 tablespoons lemon juice instead of the 1½ cups yogurt called for. Alternatively, you could use 2 tablespoons apple cider vinegar diluted with 2 tablespoons water, adding this to 6 cups milk.

⊛ To make a smaller batch of paneer, use 4 cups milk with 1 cup plain yogurt or 2 to 3 tablespoons freshly squeezed lemon juice. With yogurt, you will get about 6 ounces or 1½ cups loosely packed ½-inch cubes of paneer; with lemon juice, you will get about 4 ounces or 1 cup loosely packed ½-inch cubes.

TAMARIND LIQUID

Makes about ⅓ cup

TAMARIND LIQUID is made by soaking the dark, sticky, smoke-flavored pulp of tamarind pods in warm water and then straining out the fibers and seeds. Tamarind's sour taste is fruity, somewhere between the sweetness of raisins and the sharp edge of lemon and lime. Asian cooks use it in savory dishes.

1   heaping tablespoon of tamarind pulp *(page 193)*, about the size of a walnut

⅓   cup warm water

Combine the tamarind and water in a deep bowl. Using your fingers, mash the tamarind pulp to begin dissolving it into the water. Let it stand for about 20 minutes, mashing it occasionally, until the tamarind softens and the water turns a rich, coffee-colored brown.

Pour the tamarind mixture through a strainer into a medium bowl, and work the contents of the strainer vigorously with the back of a spoon, pressing, scraping and mashing to extract as much essence as possible from the pulp. Scrape down the outside of the strainer basket, which will be covered with thick, rich goo. When the strainer basket contains mostly seed pods and fibers, discard the contents and stir the tamarind liquid. Its texture and consistency will be much like pea soup.

Use within a few hours, or cover and refrigerate for up to 2 days.

◀◀◀◀ ▶▶▶▶

NOTE

 If you need larger batches of tamarind liquid, use these amounts: 2 tablespoons tamarind pulp with ⅔ cup warm water to make about ½ cup tamarind liquid; 3 tablespoons tamarind pulp with 1 cup warm water to make about ¾ cup tamarind liquid.

GLOSSARY

THE FOLLOWING SECTION OFFERS background information on herbs, spices and other ingredients you will use to prepare the recipes in this book. Depending on which spices you need, you may find them in supermarkets, health-food stores, specialty-food shops or Indian and Asian markets, or you can send for them by mail (pages 257-260). For maximum flavor and aroma, buy whole spices and grind them to a powder as you need them. Preground spices are a good second choice, but keep in mind that they deteriorate quickly; use the freshest you can find. If you have ground spices from the distant past sitting on your pantry shelf, consider tossing them onto your compost heap. Then treat yourself to a fresh, fragrant supply.

Asafetida: This pungent, pale yellow seasoning is considered essential in traditional Indian cooking, particularly in vegetarian kitchens. Treasured in Southeast Asia for the appealing, onionlike flavor and aroma it takes on after it is cooked and for its power to aid digestion by tempering the gassy properties of beans and legumes, it is added to many legume dishes as a matter of course. Known in Hindi as *hing*, asafetida is a dried, powdered resin from the roots of plants in the fennel family and is grown and processed in India, Afghanistan and Iran. It remains an acquired taste in the West, primarily due to its strong, sulfury smell. Look for it in Indian markets or send for it by mail (see pages 257-260). You may find it sold in lumps, to be crushed to powder as needed, but it is more commonly available in powdered form. Keep it sealed airtight, enclosing its container within another jar if you find its pervasive aroma taking over your spice shelf. Asafetida is used in small quantities and keeps for many months, so a small amount will serve you for some time. There is no substitute, but it can be omitted from recipes if you wish. I like its intense and unusual flavor.

Atta: This Indian-style whole-wheat flour milled to a fine, soft powder is used in chapatis, pooris and other traditional flat-breads. You can purchase atta from Indian markets, or mix equal amounts of whole-wheat flour and white flour together and use that mixture in place of it. Western-style whole-wheat flour is a poor substitute since it is usually higher in gluten and always a much coarser grind, yielding a very heavy bread in Indian-style recipes. A blend of whole-wheat and white flour, however, works well in place of soft atta flour.

Basil: *see* **Thai basil.**

Basmati rice: Growing only in the foothills of the Himalayas, basmati is naturally aromatic, releasing a delicate, nutty perfume as it cooks. Its distinctively long, slender grains elongate when cooked rather than plumping up as do most varieties of rice. White basmati is traditionally used in South Asian recipes, and cooks faster than brown basmati. Basmati rice is found in Indian and Middle Eastern markets and often sold in large burlap sacks, but it is also increasingly available in 1- and 2-pound packages in supermarkets and specialty-food shops. Its rarity and the challenges of raising it make it costly compared to domestic rice, but its texture, aroma and taste are worth the price. Increasingly, the word "basmati" is being used as a generic term for any fragrant long-grain rice, including Thai jasmine rice. Jasmine rice is less expensive, cooking more like domestic long-grain rice than the needlelike basmati. I love and use both.

Black cardamom: *see* **cardamom.**

Black or brown mustard seeds: These tiny globes vary in color from black to brown to a blue-tinged purple, though "black" is the most common description you will find on labeled packets. They are first cousins of the slightly larger yellow mustard seeds, which are sometimes called "white" mustard seeds to confuse the issue further. Think of mustard seeds as dark and light to avoid getting stuck on searching for a particular shade. Both light and dark mustard seeds are ground together to make powdered mustard, the base for the condiment beloved in the Western world. Indian cooks fry black or brown mustard seeds whole until they pop open, or grind them to a powder used in spice mixtures and pastes. Also valued in regional Indian cuisines for their pungent oil and for the greens they produce when planted, dark mustard seeds can be found in Indian markets, through mail-order spice sources and in many health-food stores. Though they differ somewhat in flavor, light mustard seeds make a good substitute for dark ones.

Cardamom: These plump, teardrop-shaped pods season both sweet and savory dishes in India and Sri Lanka. They are used occasionally in Southeast Asian cooking, particularly in mussamun curries and other dishes of clearly Indian origin. You will find cardamom in three forms: whole, papery, green or white pods; tiny, dark, gravel-like seeds extracted from their pods; and seeds ground to a fine gray powder. The pods come in green, white and black. Green and white cardamom pods are more widely available in the West, perhaps because of their use in baking. White cardamom pods are in fact green ones that have been bleached, a process that diminishes their aroma and flavor. Black cardamom is larger and sold only as whole pods, primarily by markets and mail-order sources specializing in Indian ingredients. Although they differ in flavor, black, green and white cardamom pods can be substituted for one another in curry recipes. I prefer the green to white because it is in its most natural state and is easier to find than black. Each cardamom pod contains around 20 seeds; 8 pods yield about ½ teaspoon cardamom seeds or ground cardamom.

Chili garlic sauce: This Chinese/Vietnamese condiment is widely available in Asian markets and in some supermarkets. The kind I love is labeled *tuong ot toi* Viet Nam. It comes in a plastic bottle with a parrot-green top and is a rich, thick, red puree of chilies with visible seeds and the texture of tomato sauce. For mail-order sources, see pages 258 and 259. If chili garlic sauce is not available, coarsely ground chili pepper or Tabasco sauce will make tasty alternatives.

Chili peppers: These pungent herbs thrive in the warm sun and are used to heat up savory dishes all over the world. Chilies follow a simple rule: Smaller means hotter. Big, green bell peppers have no heat at all; long, thick, green Anaheim chilies are mildly hot; plump yellow Hungarian wax peppers have a minor bite; plump, thumb-size jalapeños and pinkie-size serranos have lots of fire; and tiny Thai bird peppers, called *prik kii noo*, are miniature dynamite sticks. Like fresh peppers, dried red peppers are widely available in supermarkets, but you can also buy them through mail-order sources and in Indian, Asian and Mexican markets. *Chiles de arbol* and *chiles japones* are finger-length hot varieties that are fairly easy to find. Larger varieties, such as New Mexico and California chilies, tend to be milder and sweeter.

Chinese parsley: *see* **cilantro.**

Cilantro: Also known as Chinese parsley and fresh coriander, this herb has flat leaves resembling Italian parsley in shape, though they are a brighter green with a more delicate texture. Cilantro is used lavishly as a garnish as well as a source of flavor and aroma in all kinds of savory Asian dishes. Its intense fragrance fades quickly, so it is often chopped and added just before serving. Its importance in Mexican cooking makes it widely available in supermarkets in many parts of the U.S., as well as in Indian and Asian markets. Buy bunches with roots attached when you can, both because they will keep a few days longer than rootless cilantro and because the roots are used in

Thai-style curry pastes, where they add moisture and a mild, herbaceous note. Store in the refrigerator, roots in water and leaves loosely covered with a plastic bag, for up to 1 week. Plant coriander seeds in your garden if you want to grow a patch at home. Note that coriander grows quickly but tends to bolt, so you may want to keep a new crop going to have an ongoing supply of leaves. There is no substitute, but you can use an equal amount of whatever fresh green herbs you have available for an herbal infusion with a different flavor. If you need cilantro roots for Thai curry pastes and cannot find them, chopped stems and leaves make an acceptable substitute. Never substitute ground coriander seed for cilantro leaves or roots, as it bears no culinary resemblance to fresh.

Cinnamon: Queen of the sweet spices, cinnamon has been treasured since biblical times for its inviting aroma and intense flavor. The petite, rust-colored scrolls of delicate bark come from a tropical evergreen tree in the laurel family that is cultivated in India, Sri Lanka, Madagascar and the Seychelles. Cinnamon is used whole in Indian-style curries and pilafs to infuse a delicate level of seasoning and to provide visual pleasure. Cinnamon sticks are ground up into garam masala and other spice mixtures for savory South Asian dishes. Cinnamon can be found in stick form in many supermarkets, specialty-food stores, Indian and Mexican markets and mail-order outlets. To turn whole sticks, which are 3 or more inches long, into powder, wrap them in a tea towel and crush them with a kitchen mallet or an unopened can. Then transfer the shards to a heavy mortar or a coffee grinder dedicated to spice grinding and grind to a fine powder.

Cloves: One of four essential ingredients in garam masala, cloves are tiny chocolate-brown spikes, known in Spanish as *clavos*, meaning "nails." Extraordinarily aromatic and flavorful, they are tiny flower buds of a tropical evergreen tree flourishing near the sea in Indonesia, Madagascar, Zanzibar and the West

Indies. Cloves were valued in ancient China as well as India. In Western kitchens, they perfume sweets and add flavor and beauty to baked ham. Harvested by hand just before they bloom, these tiny scepters infuse pilafs and curries with their robust flavor. Cloves are widely available in supermarkets as well as from spice vendors.

Coconut milk: Used often in Thai cooking as a luxurious sauce base for spicy curry pastes, coconut milk has countless uses in Southeast Asian cuisine. The milk is made from the firm, white flesh of the dried coconut, which is extracted from its hairy brown shell, ground, soaked in water and then squeezed and strained to extract a rich, almost sweet essence. Look for unsweetened coconut milk in cans imported from Thailand and in plump plastic bags in the freezer section of Asian markets. Unsweetened coconut milk is as thick as cream when used straight from the can, so thin it with water or broth to the consistency you want. It tends to separate as it stands. When you open a can,

you may find a top layer of pure white, creamy coconut essence that is as thick as butter and below it, a thin, watery, bluish gray liquid. This separation is normal and will occur unless the can has been stored in a very warm place. If you are adding the entire can all at once to a curry or soup, you need not mix the contents beforehand, but if you are adding part of it, stir with a fork first. You can substitute cashew milk (page 233), soy milk or dairy milk if you like, with different but acceptable results. Avoid Coco Lopez and other canned sweetened coconut milk brands, which are intended for use in preparing piña coladas and other "tropical" drinks; their intense sweetness makes them unacceptable for curries and other savory Asian dishes.

Coriander: The seed of the herb that is also known as cilantro, Chinese parsley and fresh coriander, this spice consists of small, thinly veined, straw-colored globes about half the size of peppercorns. Widely available both whole and ground in supermarkets, specialty-food shops and

Indian and Asian markets, it is ubiquitous in curry pastes, curry powders and an enormous range of savory dishes in India, Thailand and neighboring countries. Coriander is easy to grow, particularly in spring and fall. Once it goes to seed, harvest the seeds on their stalks, gather them into little sheaves and hang them upside down to dry.

Cumin: These tiny, sharp seeds of Middle Eastern origin are pale gray-green when raw and a handsome straw-colored brown when dry-roasted. Related to parsley, cumin seeds bear a resemblance to the larger, plumper fennel and caraway seeds, though each has a completely different taste. Essential to Tex-Mex chili-powder mixtures in Western cooking, cumin seeds are used extensively in curries and other dishes of India and Southeast Asia. Whole cumin is toasted in oil and cooked with basmati rice, and dry-roasted cumin is ground and added to yogurt raitas for a spicy bite. You will find cumin whole and ground on most supermarket spice shelves, and you will often be instructed

to roast it to develop its flavor. There is no substitute.

Curry leaves: These shiny, emerald-green leaves that smell and taste like curry powder are used in savory dishes in Indian kitchens, particularly in the southern part of the country. I have seen them sold fresh, attached to a slender, foot-long stem, in a wholesale produce market in Los Angeles. You are more likely to find them dried, off the stem and inevitably diminished in flavor in Indian markets and by mail-order. Add them if you have them, but simply omit them if you do not, as there is no real substitute. While they are a treat, they are a bonus rather than an essential source of flavor.

Curry paste: Curry paste is a wet *masala* (which means "a mixture of spices"), with fragrant herbs and pungent spices ground together. Indian curry pastes usually include onion, garlic, fresh ginger, chili peppers and roasted ground spices, seasoned with a tangy jolt of tamarind and preserved in oil. Thai curry pastes use more chili peppers, shallots, garlic, lemongrass and galanga and more toasted cumin, coriander and peppercorns. You can make your own Thai curry pastes or purchase prepared pastes through mail-order sources, at Indian and Asian markets and, increasingly, in specialty-food shops and supermarkets. They generally keep for up to 2 months in the refrigerator and several months longer in the freezer.

Curry powder: A shortcut generic spice blend popular since the time of the British Raj, curry powder includes coriander, cumin, fenugreek, chili peppers, peppercorns, cinnamon, cardamom and turmeric. It is widely available in supermarkets and specialty-food stores. Check Asian markets for hot, tasty blends imported from Singapore and Malaysia, or assemble spices and roast and grind your own aromatic curry powder at home.

Dal: This word is commonly used to refer to lentils, dried beans and split peas in their many colorful and distinctive forms. It also refers to the lentil stews and porridges that are a part of every traditional Indian meal, from the simplest supper to the most elaborate feast. You can find brown lentils in most supermarkets along with black-eyed peas, chickpeas and other dried beans. Health-food stores are an excellent source for more exotic lentils and split peas, which are commonly referred to as pulses in Great Britain and English-speaking India. Indian markets and mail-order sources will supply you with the most complete selection of dals used in Indian cooking. Since they keep beautifully, you can stock up and keep a supply on hand if they are difficult to find near your home. Following are the most common kinds of dal used in Indian and other traditional curry cooking:

Channa dal: A variety of chickpea, it is smaller and plumper, oval rather than round, and has a pale yellow color. Its flavor and texture are richer than that of lentils, luxurious and a bit peanutty. Also called Bengal gram, channa dal is ground into chickpea flour, called *besan*.

Masoor dal: Also called red lentil, this small split pea is actually salmon-pink to orange in color. It cooks quickly, turning from a sunset hue to a dusky yellow in the process.

Moong dal: Widely used in East Asian as well as South Asian cooking, this is better known as the mung bean. In China, moong dal is sprouted to produce the familiar Chinese-style bean sprout. It is also ground into flour to make delicate bean thread noodles, also called cellophane noodles and glass noodles because of their transparency once cooked. Moong dal is sold three ways: unhulled with the dark green to khaki-colored husks intact; split with hulls on; and hulled, leaving only the petite bright yellow oval centers. This tasty dal cooks quickly and is easily digested, making it traditional fare for the very young, the very old and those who are ill.

Toovar dal: Also called arhar dal, red gram dal and pigeon pea, this large, oddly rounded yellowish pea is popular in southern and western regions of India. Often rubbed with oil as a preservative measure, it may need to be briefly soaked and rinsed to remove this soft sheen.

Urad dal: Also called black gram dal, this seed has a black hull and may be sold whole and unhulled, split with hulls left on, or hulled, leaving only its cream-colored interior. This dal costs a bit more than the others and takes longer to cook. It is used in curries and bean dishes, as well as being the key ingredient in rice and lentil pancakes, called dosas, and crisp lentil wafers, called pappadums.

Dried Chinese mushrooms: These woody mushrooms are dry as a bone, yet explode with deep, autumnal flavor once they are soaked until soft. Used in Chinese soups and stir-fries, they fortify vegetarian dishes. *See* **shiitake mushrooms.**

Fennel: These licorice-flavored seeds look like fat, greenish relatives of cumin, but the resemblance is only skin-deep. A minor player in the Indian spice lineup, fennel is used often in the cooking of Kashmir and in the condiments of other regions. Fennel is basic to *panch poran*, a classic mixture of five spices, and to the blend of whole spices called *pa'an*, which is offered to cleanse and sweeten the palate after meals.

Fenugreek: This flat, squarish little spice is both a seed and a bean. In India, fenugreek is not only toasted and ground as a spice but also planted to produce edible greens that are eaten both raw and cooked. Sprouted fenugreek is good in salads. Fenugreek is a basic ingredient in curry powder, contributing to its flavor and aroma. Known in Hindi as *methi*, whole fenugreek seeds are used extensively in traditional Indian kitchens both for their flavor and as a source of protein and vitamins in vegetarian cuisine. The seeds are usually dry-roasted or fried in oil briefly. This step tempers their bitter and rather overpowering flavor and enhances their nutty aroma.

Fish sauce: This clear, whiskey-colored condiment is ubiquitous in Thailand, where it is called *nahm plah*; in Vietnam, where it is called *nuoc mam*; and in the Philippines, where it is called *patis*. Also used extensively in Laos, Cambodia and Burma, it is a pungent essence of anchovies and other tiny saltwater fish. It smells mighty fishy, but its taste softens considerably as it cooks, and it is indispensable in traditional Southeast Asian cooking, where its role is comparable to that of soy sauce in Japanese, Korean and Chinese kitchens. To substitute, add a dash of soy sauce and salt to taste.

Fresh coriander: *see* **cilantro.**

Galanga: Sometimes called Siamese or Thai ginger, this pungent member of the ginger family is also called Java root, *galingale, galangal, rieng, laos* and *lenguas*. Its Thai name is *kha*. A rhizome or underground stem, it is ivory-colored inside and out, with thin, dark rings encircling its shiny surface. Its plump fingers are studded with drying stubs of the green leafy shoots it sends up as it grows underground, parallel to the surface. Thais mince galanga and pound it with chilies, lemongrass, garlic, shallots and spices to make their explosively delicious curry pastes. You will find it in Asian markets in four forms: fresh in "hands," like ginger; frozen in plastic packets; dried in woody chips in cellophane packets; and ground to a powder. Choose galanga in this order, omitting the powdered form since it retains so little flavor and aroma that it is useless. Ginger makes an acceptable substitute, though its flavor is sweeter and lacks the lemon-lime bite of its cousin. Trim away any hard, dry or brown portions before slicing and mincing fresh galanga. You need not peel it.

Garam masala: *see* **masala.**

Ghee: This pure butterfat is rendered by heating butter slowly over a low flame. The process causes the water to evaporate and the milk solids to separate, forming a crusty layer on top and sinking to the bottom, where they brown. It is then removed, leaving behind a clear, golden oil with a scrumptious nutty taste. Unlike butter, ghee keeps for months without refrigeration and can be used to fry onions, rice and other ingredients at high temperatures and for long periods of time. Reheat it gently if

it solidifies. Ghee endows onions, rice and other ingredients with its rich, toasty flavor. See pages 257 and 258 for mail-order sources, and page 234 to make ghee at home.

Ginger, fresh: Rotund little clusters, or "hands," of fresh ginger now grace the produce sections of many supermarkets, a tribute to the popularity of Chinese cuisine in the West. Ginger is used lavishly in Indian and Thai kitchens as well as in tropical countries throughout the world where the ginger plant thrives. A rhizome, or underground stem, ginger is grown for export in Hawaii and Fiji and is used fresh in curries, curry pastes, sautéed dishes and soups in South Asian and Southeast Asian kitchens. Look for shiny hunks that are heavy for their size and seem ready to burst from their skins. Avoid those that are beginning to shrivel. Keep ginger at room temperature in a basket on the counter with your fresh garlic, chilies, shallots and onions, so that you will use it often. Or refrigerate, whole and unpeeled, for several weeks in the vegetable crisper. To mince fresh ginger, peel a lump several inches long and slice crosswise as thinly as possible. Stack the slices, cut them into thin strips, then cut the strips crosswise into tiny pieces.

Ginger, dried and powdered: A sweet spice used extensively in baking in the West, this moist, pale yellow powder is widely available in supermarkets. It is common in curry powders. Because it changes character while drying, it cannot substitute for fresh ginger.

Green cardamom: *see* **cardamom.**

Green onion: Also called scallions and spring onions, these fragrant vegetables are sold in bunches with long, green shoots extending from a white, sometimes bulbous base with the roots attached. Refrigerate until needed, trim away the roots, the outermost layer of skin and any tired or discolored greens, and chop as needed for use in cooking or as a garnish.

Indian-style curry paste: *see* **curry paste.**

Jaggery: *see* **palm sugar.**

Jasmine rice: A naturally aromatic long-grain white variety, jasmine rice is grown in central and northeastern Thailand and exported to demanding rice lovers around the world. Traditionally cooked with water alone as a bland foil to the intensely flavored dishes composing a Thai meal, jasmine rice is available in Asian markets, through mail-order sources and, increasingly, in supermarkets. Like basmati, jasmine rice is unsuited to growing conditions in the West, but a number of hybrid strains, including texmati, jazmati, wild pecan and popcorn rice, are now grown in the U.S.

Kaffir or kefir lime leaves: *see* **wild lime leaves.**

Lemongrass: Shaped like sturdy, fibrous green onions, lemongrass has long, slender stalks endowed with a lemony flavor and scent. But whereas lemon is sharp-edged and brassy tasting, lemongrass has a cool, soft, delicate citrus taste. Its grassy, pale to medium green tops grow out of a whitish, bulbous base with an interior purple tinge. A basic ingredient in Thai curry pastes, fresh lemongrass is increasingly available in supermarkets and farmers' markets in the West, as well as in Asian markets. It is easy to grow if you can find a healthy bunch of stalks. Cut away tops to leave a 6-inch base and place it in water for a few weeks. When you have fat, white roots and long, hairy roots, plant in pots, or outdoors in temperate climates, making sure they get lots of sun and some water. Plant in V-shaped pairs, so that new growth can shoot up and fill in around the parent stalks. Dried lemongrass has virtually no flavor; avoid it. In curry pastes, you can substitute a teaspoon of lemon zest for each stalk with acceptable results, if fresh lemongrass is difficult to find. But for Thai-style soups, which are infused with whole stalks, you need fresh.

Mace: Mace and nutmeg come from the peachlike fruit of a tropical evergreen. Mace is the bright red, lacy covering that encircles the nutmeg seed. Sometimes available dried whole, it is widely found in ground form. In flavor it is similar to nutmeg. It has savory uses in India, France and Britain, though its most common use in the West is in sweets.

Masala: *Masala* is a Hindi word meaning "a mixture of spices." Dry masalas are composed of whole spices, often dry-roasted before they are ground to a powder. Wet masalas—the curry foundation of choice throughout Southeast Asia, particularly in Thailand, Laos, Cambodia, Malaysia and Singapore—are composed of the dry spices pounded together with finely chopped fresh herbs, such as garlic, onion, ginger, lemongrass, chilies and cilantro, to make a moist paste. Dry masalas are sprinkled on curries during and after cooking, and wet masalas are sautéed in oil or coconut milk as a first step. Traditionally, both kinds of masalas are cooked before they are eaten to smooth the raw edges of the spices and marry them with one another and with the herbs. Garam masala is a dry preparation made of cinnamon, peppercorns, cloves and other spices. *Garam* means "warming" in Hindi, a reference not to the fiery heat of chili peppers but to the gentle warming effect of the spice mixture on the body. It is used in small amounts, added during cooking and often sprinkled over a curry dish just before it is served.

Mung beans: *see* **dal (moong).**

Mustard seeds: *see* **black or brown mustard seeds.**

Nutmeg: Though it is widely available dried and retains its flavor and aroma better than most spices after grinding, try to buy nutmeg whole and grate it as needed. Check specialty-food shops if you want a small grater designed for nutmeg, or chop it and grind it in a mortar, or grate it on a box grater. In Indian cooking, nutmeg is used in garam masala and in some savory dishes. *See also* **mace.**

Palm sugar: A soft, sticky brown sugar, also known as coconut sugar and coconut candy, palm sugar is extracted from the sap of both palmyra and coconut palm trees and is used extensively in Southeast Asian cooking. Look for it in Asian markets and mail-order catalogs. It ranges in color from light beige to deep reddish brown and in texture from a sensuous, shiny goo to moist, grainy clumps to rock-hard stuff that is difficult to extract from the jar. I prefer to buy palm sugar in cans, because it is almost always moist and usable. Palm sugar is similar to and interchangeable in most recipes with jaggery, a brown sugar used in Indian kitchens. Either light or dark brown sugar makes an adequate substitute.

Paneer cheese: This fresh, soft, white cheese is essential in such dishes as mattar paneer, a delectable curry of green peas and tomatoes studded with crisp fried chunks of paneer. It is unavailable commercially but easy to make at home using milk and yogurt or lemon juice (see page 236). You can substitute pressed tofu for paneer in many recipes with good results.

Paprika: A mild, red chili pepper widely available ground to a dry powder. Paprika is used primarily for its crimson color.

Red lentils: *see* **dal (masoor).**

Scallion: *see* **green onion.**

Shallots: Petite members of the onion family with reddish brown, papery skin, shallots are used lavishly in the cooking of South Asia and Southeast Asia. Sliced crosswise, they sport a delicate purple lining on their moist interior segments. They can be as small as walnuts or large enough to fill your palm. Look for plump, shiny shallots that are heavy for their size. Store them with their cousins garlic and onions at room temperature and exposed to air. Those with green shoots peeking out of their stem end should be your last choice, as their flavor is being sacrificed to the growth of the next generation. Use them if they are all you find, or separate them into bulbs and plant them in your garden. Onions make an acceptable substitute.

Shiitake mushrooms: Large, delicious mushrooms with flat, chocolate-colored caps and café-au-lait gills and stems. The shiitake is tasty when fresh and incredibly flavorful when dried. Its name is Japanese, and it is one of many mushrooms dried and used in East Asian cooking. To use dried shiitakes and other dried mushrooms, soak in warm water for 20 to 30 minutes. Strain the water through a coffee filter if you wish to use it for its flavor, as it will contain some grit. Chop the softened mushrooms as directed. *See* **dried Chinese mushrooms.**

Siamese ginger: *see* **galanga.**

Tamarind: The sticky, coffee-colored fruit of the beautiful tamarind tree, this seasoning grows in big, beany pods, which are often available fresh in Asian, Caribbean and Hispanic markets. Tamarind pulp is soaked in warm water, mashed to release its flavor and to separate the fruit from the seeds, then strained to leave a heavenly, sweet-and-sour essence that adds immensely to the flavor of any dish in which it is used. It's a mess to work with, but it's worth it. Look for small, dark blocks of tamarind pulp in Asian markets. These will keep for years at room temperature. The tamarind liquid you make from it will keep refrigerated for about a week or frozen for several months. Freshly squeezed lime or lemon juice and some sugar is a fair substitute for its smoky tang.

Thai basil: Asian markets carry a Southeast Asian cousin of Italian basil, with a stronger licorice flavor and with purple stems and flowers. Its Thai name is *bai horapah*, and its Vietnamese name is *rau que*. Italian basil makes a good substitute.

Thai chilies: *see* **chili peppers.**

Thai-style curry paste: *see* **curry paste.**

Turmeric: This cousin of the ginger family is prized throughout Asia for its deep golden color. Turmeric is treasured as a natural dye and was originally used to color the orange robes worn by Theravada Buddhist monks. Turmeric has been used for centuries in an array of foods, including rice, curries and fish dishes, and is valued for its antiseptic properties, both in food preparation and in traditional medicine. It is the secret of the vivid yellow of both curry powder and ballpark mustard. Turmeric is a rhizome, which is a stem that tunnels along underground, growing parallel to the surface and sending hairlike roots down into the dirt and gorgeous tall ginger flowers up into the sun. It can be found fresh in many Asian markets. Look for small, fingerlike herbs resembling ginger in their rounded shape and smooth texture. On the outside, the knobs are a dull, soft brown, masking a moist, fibrous flesh of a brilliant carroty orange. Dried turmeric is more available than fresh and just as good. Turmeric has a faint earthy flavor; its main job is to color rather than season. It will temporarily stain fingers, cutting boards and anything else it touches.

White cardamom: *see* **cardamom.**

Wild lime leaves: These brilliant green citrus leaves add their sharp flavor and aroma to Thai-style curries and soups. Also known as kaffir or kefir lime leaves, they adorn the thorny branches of a tropical tree known as *Citrus hystrix.* Although wild lime leaves cannot be imported from Southeast Asia due to agricultural restrictions, they have been grown in the U.S. for years and are sold fresh and frozen in Asian markets. Dried wild lime leaves are also available, but as they retain only a whisper of their perfume, they make a poor substitute for fresh. Traditionally, the sturdy leaves are left in the dish but not eaten, though cooks sometimes slice them crosswise into delicate threads, which are sprinkled over curries. Wild lime leaves freeze well, so buy extra, seal them airtight, and keep in the freezer for six months or so. Add the frozen leaves to soups and curries without thawing. Because frozen leaves have less flavor than fresh, you may want to use twice the amount when substituting them. If you cannot locate wild lime leaves, omit them.

Wild rice: Botanically speaking, wild rice is different from the family of grains we call rice, but from a cook's perspective, it is similar to its culinary cousins. Its ebony grains are straight and sharp as needles, and they need longer and more vigorous cooking than other types of rice in order to become tender. Boil wild rice in lots of salted water and drain it well once it splits open and is tender, 45 minutes to an hour. Cooked wild rice is plump and chewy, and when its grains burst, they reveal a creamy core. Wild rice has an earthy, nutty flavor and aroma. You will find it in specialty-food shops, many supermarkets and through mail-order food sources. It keeps well for many months, so lay in a supply if it is difficult to find. The finest wild rice is still harvested by Native Americans in the marshlands of Minnesota. Its cost reflects the time and care taken to gather the grains by hand from a canoe in the traditional way.

MAIL-ORDER SOURCES

INGREDIENTS

ADRIANA'S CARAVAN
409 Vanderbilt Street
Brooklyn, NY 11218
(718) 436-8565
(800) 316-0820

A cornucopia of ingredients and equipment for cooking food from around the world, with particular emphasis on Southeast Asian and South Asian cuisines. In addition to carrying an extensive stock of dried herbs and spices, including asafetida, this vendor will ship fresh herbs to you, including lemongrass, wild lime leaves, curry leaves, galanga and Thai basil. Owner Rochelle Zabarkes also carries ethnic cooking utensils, including the handsome granite mortar and pestle sets made in Thailand, which are ideal for grinding curry pastes at home. For grinding whole spices, she sells traditional spice grinders made of brass, imported from Italy and the Middle East.

GOLD MINE NATURAL FOOD
COMPANY
3419 Hancock Street
San Diego, CA 92110-4307
(800) 475-3663
(619) 296-9756

Organic rice, other grains, flours, couscous, noodles, lentils, beans, seeds and nuts, dried mushrooms and cooking utensils.

HOUSE OF SPICES
82-80 Broadway
Jackson Heights, NY 11373
(718) 476-1577

Extensive selection of Indian and Pakistani foodstuffs, including asafetida and other whole and ground spices, brown and white basmati rice, lentils, beans, nuts, seeds, atta flour, chutneys, pickles, pappadums, dried fruit, cooking oils, dairy ghee, vegetable ghee, tamarind, curry pastes and powders and traditional Indian cooking utensils.

INDIAN GROCERIES AND SPICES
10633 West North Avenue
Wauwatosa, WI 53226
(414) 771-3535

Extensive selection of Indian and Pakistani foodstuffs, including asafetida, which is listed under its Hindi name, *hing*. The store also carries whole and ground spices, basmati rice, jasmine rice, lentils, beans, nuts and seeds, atta flour, chutneys, pickles, pappadums, dried fruit, cooking oils, dairy ghee, vegetable ghee, tamarind, curry pastes and powders and traditional Indian cooking utensils.

OASIS
4130 Rochester Road
Royal Oak, MI 48073
(810) 588-2210
Fax (810) 588-1654

Spices, curry pastes, powders, pickles, chutneys and condiments.

THE ORIENTAL PANTRY
423 Great Road
Acton, MA 01720
(800) 828-0368
(508) 264-4576
Fax (617) 275-4506
Internet: http://www.top.com

Extensive ingredients, equipment and serving dishes for East, South and Southeast Asian cuisines, including rice, noodles, some spices, dried mushrooms, fish sauce, soy sauce, chili garlic sauce, unsweetened coconut milk, Thai- and Indian-style curry pastes, tamarind pulp, chutneys, pickles and pappadums.

PENZEYS, LTD.
P.O. Box 1448
Waukesha, WI 53187-9820
(414) 574-0277
Fax (414) 574-0278

A superb collection of spices for cooking the cuisines of the world, including those of South and Southeast Asia. The handsome catalog is a terrific read, and their spices are excellent. I generally avoid dried lemongrass and dried galanga, as they lose flavor and aroma quickly once they begin to dry, and most of what you will find in the marketplace is stale and tasteless. Penzeys provides dried versions of these two herbs that still have much of their magic, so if you cannot obtain these herbs fresh, this is a good alternative.

PURITY FARMS, INC.
14635 Westcreek Road
Sedalia, CO 80135
(303) 647-2368
Fax (303) 647-9875

Ghee made from grade AA certified organic butter with no BHT or other hormones. Also natural kosher ghee.

SPICE MERCHANT
P.O. Box 524
Jackson Hole, WY 83001
(800) 551-5999
(307) 733-7811

Extensive ingredients, equipment and serving dishes for East, South and Southeast Asian cuisines, including rice, noodles, some spices, dried mushrooms, fish sauce, soy sauce, chili garlic sauce, coconut milk, palm sugar, Thai- and Indian-style curry pastes, tamarind pulp, chutneys and pickles and pappadums. The Spice Merchant carries mortar and pestle sets made of both marble and porcelain, suitable for grinding whole spices to a powder as well as beautiful brass spice mills imported from the Middle East.

SULTAN'S DELIGHT
P.O. Box 090302
Brooklyn, NY 11209
(800) 852-5046
(718) 745-2121
Fax (718) 745-2563

Whole and ground spices, grains, lentils, beans, seeds and nuts, chutney and fish sauce.

COOKBOOKS

THAI KITCHEN
EPICUREAN INTERNATIONAL
P.O. Box 13242
Berkeley, CA 94712
(800) 967-THAI
(510) 268-0209
Fax (510) 834-3102

Basic ingredients for cooking Thai and Southeast Asian food, including jasmine rice, curry pastes, palm sugar, fish sauce and unsweetened coconut milk.

WALNUT ACRES INC.
P.O. Box 8
Penns Creek, PA 17862
(800) 433-3998
Fax (717) 837-1146

Organic rice, other grains, flours, couscous, lentils, beans, seeds and nuts.

BOOKS FOR COOKS
4 Blenheim Crescent
London
W11-1NN, United Kingdom
Telephone: 0171-221-1992
Fax: 0171-221-1517

An excellent source for cookbooks and other food books published outside the United States. They reply quickly to faxed inquiries and accept major credit cards.

KITCHEN ARTS AND LETTERS
1435 Lexington Avenue
(between 93rd and 94th streets)
New York, NY 10128
(212) 876-5550

An excellent source for cookbooks on a wide range of topics and a diligent search service for out-of-print or otherwise difficult-to-obtain books.

BIBLIOGRAPHY

I HAVE FOUND THE FOLLOWING BOOKS HELPFUL in learning about the flavorful and fragrant world of spices, curries and the dishes that accompany them. Check with the cookbook vendors listed in Mail-Order Sources (previous page) for information on books that are published outside the United States or are out of print.

Achaya, K.T. *Indian Food: A Historical Companion.* Delhi: Oxford University Press, 1994.

Africa News Service, Tami Hultman, Ed. *The Africa News Cookbook.* New York: Viking Penguin, 1985.

Alford, Jeffrey and Naomi Duguid. *Flatbreads and Flavors: A Baker's Atlas.* New York: William Morrow, 1995.

Arora, Renu. *Cooking with Curry.* Tokyo: Shufunotomo, 1985.

Balasuriya, Heather Janz and Karin Winegar. *Fire & Spice: The Cuisine of Sri Lanka.* New York: McGraw-Hill, 1989.

Batra, Neelam. *The Indian Vegetarian.* New York: Macmillan, 1994.

Bhumichitr, Vatcharin. *The Essential Thai Cookbook.* New York: Clarkson Potter, 1994.

Bhumichitr, Vatcharin. *The Taste of Thailand.* New York: Atheneum, 1988.

Brennan, Jennifer. *The Original Thai Cookbook.* New York: Times Books, 1981.

Brennan, Jennifer. *Curries and Bugles: A Memoir and Cookbook of the British Raj.* New York: HarperCollins, 1990.

Carey, Phillis M. *The Casual Gourmet: 50 Easy Entertaining Menus.* Carlsbad, CA: Spoon and Whisk Productions, 1993.

Chapman, Pat. *The Curry Club Book of Indian Cuisine.* Rocklin, CA.: Prima Publishing, 1992.

Chatterjee, Sandeep. *The Spice Trail: 100 Hot Dishes from India to Indonesia.* Berkeley: Ten Speed Press, 1995.

Cost, Bruce. *Bruce Cost's Asian Ingredients.* New York: William Morrow, 1988.

Day, Harvey. *Curries of the Orient*. London: Heritage Publishers, 1972.

DeWitt, Dave and Arthur J. Pais. *A World of Curries*. New York: Little, Brown, 1994.

Fraser, Linda. *The Book of Curries and Indian Foods*. Los Angeles: HP Books, 1989.

Grigson, Sophie. *Gourmet Ingredients*. New York: Van Nostrand Reinhold, 1991.

Harris, Jessica B. *Iron Pots and Wooden Spoons: Africa's Gifts to New World Cooking*. New York: Atheneum, 1989.

Harris, Jessica B. *Sky Juice and Flying Fish: Traditional Caribbean Cooking*. New York: Fireside, 1991.

Jaffrey, Madhur. *An Invitation to Indian Cooking*. New York: Vintage Books, 1975.

Jaffrey, Madhur. *A Taste of India*. New York: Atheneum, 1988.

Jaffrey, Madhur. *Flavors of India*. New York: Carol Southern Books, 1995.

Khars, Kurt. *Thai Cooking*. New York: Gallery Books, 1990.

Kirchner, Bharti. *The Healthy Cuisine of India: Recipes from the Bengal Region*. Los Angeles: Lowell House, 1992.

Kirchner, Bharti. *Indian Inspired*. Chicago: Contemporary Books, 1994.

Kongpan, Sisamon and Pinyo Srisawat. *The Elegant Taste of Thailand*. Berkeley: SLG Books, 1989.

Koul, Sudha. *Curries without Worries*. Pennington, NJ: Cashmir, 1991.

Loha-Unchit, Kasma. *It Rains Fishes: Legends, Traditions and the Joy of Thai Cooking*. Rohnert Park, CA: Pomegranate Art Books, 1995.

Marks, Copeland with Mintari Soehajo. *The Indonesian Kitchen*. New York: Atheneum, 1981.

MacMillan, Maya Kaimal. *Curried Favors: Family Recipes from South India*. New York: Abbeville Press, 1996.

McNair, James. *James McNair Cooks Southeast Asian*. San Francisco: Chronicle Books, 1996.

Norman, Jill. *Spices, Roots & Fruits*. New York: Bantam Books, 1989.

Norman, Jill. *The Complete Book of Spices: A Practical Guide to Spices and Aromatic Seeds*. London: Dorling Kindersley, 1990.

Panjabi, Camellia. *50 Great Curries of India*. London: Kyle Cathie, Limited, 1994.

Pham, Mai. *The Best of Vietnamese and Thai Cooking*. Rocklin, CA: Prima Publishing, 1996.

Rani. *Feast of India*. Chicago: Contemporary Books, 1991.

Ray, Sumana. *Indian Regional Cooking*. Secaucus, NJ: Chartwell Books, 1986.

Ray, Sumana. *Indian Vegetarian Cooking*. London: Quintet Publishing, 1994.

Ross, Rosa Lo-San. *Beyond Bok Choy: A Cook's Guide to Asian Vegetables*. New York: Artisan, 1996.

Sahni, Julie. *Classic Indian Cooking*. New York: William Morrow, 1980.

Sahni, Julie. *Classic Indian Vegetarian Cooking*. New York: William Morrow, 1985.

Sahni, Julie. *Savoring Spices and Herbs: Recipe Secrets of Flavor, Aroma and Color*. New York: William Morrow, 1996.

Santa Maria, Jack. *Indian Vegetarian Cookery*. York Beach, ME: Samuel Weiser, 1982.

Seed, Diane. *Favorite Indian Cooking*. Berkeley: Ten Speed Press, 1990.

Solomon, Charmaine. *The Complete Asian Cookbook*. Boston: Charles Tuttle, 1992.

Solomon, Charmaine and Reuben Solomon. *The Complete Curry Cookbook*. New York: McGraw-Hill, 1980.

Sowell, Thomas. *Migrations and Cultures: A World View*. New York: HarperCollins/ Basic Books, 1996.

Time-Life Books, Santha Rama Rau, Ed. *The Cooking of India*. New York: Time, 1969.

von Holzen, Heinz and Lother Arsana. *The Food of Indonesia*. Singapore: Periplus Editions (HK), 1995.

von Welanetz, Diana and Paul. *The Von Welanetz Guide to Ethnic Ingredients*. Los Angeles: J.P. Tarcher, 1982.

Walker, Jane. *Creative Cooking with Spices*. Secaucus, NJ: Chartwell Books, 1985.

Yeo, Chris and Joyce Jue. *The Cooking of Singapore: Great Dishes from Asia's Culinary Crossroads*. Emeryville, CA: Harlow & Ratner, 1993.

INDEX

ABOUT THE AUTHOR

A NATIONALLY RECOGNIZED AUTHORITY on the cuisines of the Far East, Nancie McDermott fell in love with curries as a Peace Corps volunteer in northeastern Thailand. She is the author of *Real Thai: The Best of Thailand's Regional Cooking* and *The 5 in 10 Pasta Cookbook* and writes regularly for *Food & Wine, Cook's Illustrated* and *Food Arts.*